John 12–21

Son of God

JOHN A. STEWART

Lamplighters International is a Christian ministry that helps individuals engage with God and His Word and equips believers to be disciple-makers.

For additional information about Lamplighters ministry resources, contact:

Lamplighters International
771 NE Harding Street, Suite 250
Minneapolis, MN USA 55413
or visit our website at
www.LamplightersUSA.org.

Product Code Jn2-NK-2P

ISBN 978-1-931372-58-9

CONTENTS

How to Use This Study

WHAT IS LAMPLIGHTERS?

Lamplighters International is an evangelical Christian ministry that publishes Christ-centered, Bible-based curriculum and trains believers to be intentional disciple makers. This Bible study, comprising ten individual lessons, is a self-contained unit and an integral part of the entire discipleship ministry. When you have completed the study, you will have a much greater understanding of a portion of God's Word, with many new truths that you can apply to your life.

HOW TO STUDY A LAMPLIGHTERS LESSON

A Lamplighters study begins with prayer, your Bible, the weekly lesson, and a sincere desire to learn more about God's Word. The questions are presented in a progressive sequence as you work through the study material. You should not use Bible commentaries or other reference books (except a dictionary) until you have completed your weekly lesson and met with your weekly group. Approaching the Bible study in this way allows you to personally encounter many valuable spiritual truths from the Word of God.

To gain the most out of the Bible study, find a quiet place to complete your weekly lesson. Each lesson will take approximately 45–60 minutes to complete. You will likely spend more time on the first few lessons until you are familiar with the format, and our prayer is that each week will bring the discovery of important life principles.

The writing space within the weekly studies provides the opportunity for you to answer questions and respond to what you have learned. Putting answers in your own words, and including Scripture references where appropriate, will help you personalize and commit to memory the truths you have learned. The answers to the questions will be found in the Scripture references at the end of each question or in the passages listed at the beginning of each lesson.

If you are part of a small group, it's a good idea to record the specific dates that you'll be meeting to do the individual lessons. Record the specific dates each time the group will be meeting next to the lesson titles on the Contents page. Additional lines have been provided for you to record when you go through this same study at a later date.

The side margins in the lessons can be used for the spiritual insights you glean from other group or class members. Recording these spiritual truths will likely be a spiritual help to you and others when you go through this study again in the future.

Audio Introduction

A brief audio introduction is available to help you learn about the historical background of the book, gain an understanding of its theme and structure, and be introduced to some of the major truths. Audio introductions are available for all Lamplighters studies and are a great resource for the group leader; they can also be used to introduce the study to your group. To access the audio introductions, go to www.LamplightersUSA.org.

"Do You Think?" Questions

Each weekly study has a few *"do you think?"* questions designed to help you to make personal applications from the biblical truths you are learning. In the first lesson the *"do you think?"* questions are placed in italic print for easy identification. If you are part of a study group, your insightful answers to these questions could be a great source of spiritual encouragement to others.

Personal Questions

Occasionally you'll be asked to respond to personal questions. If you are part of a study group you may choose not to share your answers to these questions with the others. However, be sure to answer them for your own benefit because they will help you compare your present level of spiritual maturity to the biblical principles presented in the lesson.

A Final Word

Throughout this study the masculine pronouns are frequently used in the generic sense to avoid awkward sentence construction. When the pronouns *he*, *him*, and *his* are used in reference to the Trinity (God the Father, Jesus Christ, and the Holy Spirit), they always refer to the masculine gender.

This Lamplighters study was written after many hours of careful preparation. It is our prayer that it will help you "… grow in the grace and knowledge of our Lord and Savior Jesus Christ. To Him be the glory both now and forever. Amen" (2 Peter 3:18).

What Is an Intentional Discipleship Bible Study?

The *Next Step* in Bible Study

The Lamplighters Bible study series is ideal for individual, small group, and classroom use. This Bible study is also designed for Intentional Discipleship training. An Intentional Discipleship (ID) Bible study has four key components. Individually they are not unique, but together they form the powerful core of the ID Bible study process.

1. Objective: Lamplighters is a discipleship training ministry that has a dual objective: (1) to help individuals engage with God and His Word and (2) to equip believers to be disciple-makers. The small group format provides extensive opportunity for ministry training, and it's not limited by facilities, finances, or a lack of leadership staffing.

2. Content: The Bible is the focus rather than Christian books. Answers to the study questions are included within the study guides, so the theology is in the study material, not in the leader's mind. This accomplishes two key objectives: (1) It gives the group leader confidence to lead another individual or small group without fear, and (2) it protects the small group from theological error.

3. Process: The ID Bible study process begins with an Open House, which is followed by a 6–14-week study, which is followed by a presentation of the Final Exam (see graphic on page 8). This process provides a natural environment for continuous spiritual growth and leadership development.

4. Leadership Development: As group participants grow in Christ, they naturally invite others to the groups. The leader-trainer (1) identifies and recruits new potential leaders from within the group, (2) helps them register for online discipleship training, and (3) provides in-class leadership mentoring until they are both competent and confident to lead a group according to the ID Bible study process. This leadership development process is scalable, progressive, and comprehensive.

OVERVIEW OF THE LEADERSHIP TRAINING AND DEVELOPMENT PROCESS

There are three stages of leadership training in the Intentional Discipleship process: (1) leading studies, (2) training leaders, and (3) multiplying groups (see appendix for greater detail).

Multiplying Groups

The 5 Steps of Faith for Starting Studies

Training Library

Online Resources

Leading Studies

ST-A-R-T

10 Commandments

Solving All Group Problems

Open House

Basic Training
(1x Per Year)

6-14 Week Study

Final Exam

Training Leaders

4 Responsibilities of a Trainer   *4 Levels of Student Development*

Leadership Training   *3 Diagnostic Questions*

John A. Stewart © 2017

How Can I Be Trained?

Included within this Bible study is the student workbook for Level 1 (Basic Training). Level 1 training is both free and optional. Level 1 training teaches you a simple 4-step process (ST-A-R-T) to help you prepare a life-changing Bible study and 10 proven small group leadership principles that will help your group thrive. To register for a Level 1 online training event, either as an individual or as a small group, go to www.LamplightersUSA.org/training or www.discipleUSA. org. If you have additional questions, you can also call 800-507-9516.

ONE

BEHOLD, THE KING!

The first 11 chapters of John's gospel begin with eternity past (cf. John 1:1) and end just prior to Jesus' triumphant entry into Jerusalem—an infinite length of time. This second study of John (chapters 12–21) begins six days before the Passover (John 12:1) and concludes sometime before Christ's ascension into heaven (John 21; Acts 1:3)—a period of less than 50 days.

John 12 divides easily into four sections: (1) Mary's anointing of Jesus' feet (John 12:1–11), (2) Jesus' triumphant entry into Jerusalem (John 12:12–19), (3) a small group of Greeks who request a private meeting with Jesus (John 12:20–36), and (4) Jesus' explanation as to why some people believe and others don't.

Before you begin, please ask God to reveal Himself through His Word and to transform you into the image of His Son. May God bless your diligent study of God's Word.

Lombardi Time Rule:

If the leader arrives early, he or she has time to pray, prepare the room, and greet others personally.

———

ADD GROUP INSIGHTS BELOW

1. Six days before the Passover (probably Friday or Saturday the week before the crucifixion, depending on Roman or Jewish calculation), Jesus and His disciples arrived at Bethany, a small village approximately two miles east of Jerusalem. There He was the honored guest at an evening meal (John 12:1–2). What happened at the meal that triggered the disapproval of one of the disciples (John 12:3–5)?

_____

_____

_____

_____

_____

2. Since the value of the oil Mary used was roughly equal to a common laborer's yearly wages (perhaps $20,000–$30,000 in today's dollars), Judas's comment about Mary's "wastefulness" seems justifiable. Why didn't Judas want Mary to use the oil of spikenard (NIV: "pure nard") for her expression of love and adoration of Jesus (John 12:6)?

_____

_____

_____

3. Mary's action of washing Jesus' feet is a beautiful example of uninhibited worship—an expression of adoration that is approved by God, but often condemned by man. What specific things *do you think* Mary did to express her love for Jesus and her unrestrained worship of Him (John 12:3)?

_____

_____

_____

_____

_____

4. According to 2 Samuel 24:18–25 the prophet Gad instructed King David to erect an altar for the people to worship the Lord. David chose an elevated threshing floor that was owned by a man named Araunah (the same location that Abram offered Isaac and the current location of the Islamic Dome of the Rock) who was willing to donate his property for such a worthy purpose.

a. What did David say to Araunah about the gift of the property and his (David's) worship of God (2 Samuel 24:24)?

_____

_____

_____

b. Mary gave a costly gift (perhaps an inheritance or her dowry), and David said he wouldn't give the Lord anything that didn't cost him something. What do you regularly offer the Lord as an expression of love and gratitude for what He has done for you that costs you something?

_____

_____

_____

_____

5. When the Jewish leaders learned that Jesus was at Bethany, they sought to kill both Him and Lazarus (John 12:9–11). They planned to kill Lazarus because his resurrection from the dead had become a powerful witness that was causing many Jews to place their faith in Christ (John 12:11). Apparently the Jews never considered that Jesus could raise Lazarus from the dead again.

a. If the Jewish leaders hated Jesus and the common people were afraid of the leaders (John 7:13), who joyously welcomed Jesus into Jerusalem (John 12:12–16)?

_____

_____

_____

_____

b. What didn't Jesus' disciples understand about His entrance into Jerusalem (John 12:16; Zechariah 9:9)?

_____

_____

_____

6. Some Greeks (non-Jewish, Gentile converts to Judaism) requested an interview with Jesus (John 12:20–22). Likely, they had some questions about their inclusion in the plan of God. According to Jewish law, Gentiles could worship in the temple in Jerusalem, but their access was limited to the Court of the Gentiles. At first Jesus appeared to ignore their request, but His answer provides comfort to all non-Jews about being fully accepted into God's family. What was His answer to their question (John 12:23–26, 32)?

_____

_____

_____

7. a. Jesus said, **Now My soul is troubled, and what shall I say? "Father, save Me from this hour"? But for this purpose I came to this hour** (John 12:27). What was **this hour** He wanted to be saved from (2 Corinthians 5:21; Hebrews 12:2)? For what purpose(s) did He come (John 18:37, Luke 19:10)?

_____

_____

_____

_____

b. What _do you think_ Jesus meant by the statement **Father, glorify Your Name** (John 12:28)?

_____

_____

_____

_____

8. Name at least two important results of Jesus' death on the cross (John 12:31–32).

_____

_____

_____

_____

9. Jesus told His followers to **walk while you have the light** (John 12:35) and **to believe in the light** (John 12:36).

   a. What does it mean **to walk in the light** (John 12:35, 8:12)?

   _____

   _____

   b. What happens to you if you walk in the light and then stop walking in the light (John 12:35)?

   _____

   _____

   _____

10. John 12:37 says, **But although He had done so many signs before them, they did not believe in Him.** The apostle John, writing under the inspiration of the Holy Spirit, said, **And truly Jesus did many other signs in the presence of His disciples, which are not written in this book; but these are written that you may believe that Jesus is the Christ, the Son of God, and that believing you may have life in His name** (John 20:30–31).

   a. What happened to those who did not believe in the light Christ had manifested to them (John 12:38)?

Want to learn how to disciple another person, lead a life-changing Bible study or start another study? Go to www.Lamplighters USA.org/training to learn how.

_____

ADDITIONAL INSIGHTS

_____

_____

_____

b. What happens to those to whom God does not reveal
Himself (John 12:39–41)?

_____

_____

_____

_____

11. Jesus came to save the world not to judge the world (John
12:47). Who or what will judge the world in the final judgment
(John 12:48–50)?

_____

_____

_____

_____

_____

Two

THE 11TH COMMANDMENT

Read John 13; other references as given.

Throughout John's gospel the apostle emphasizes that Jesus lived according to a divine timetable. When Jesus' mother informed Him about the shortage of wine at the wedding at Cana, He replied, **My hour has not yet come** (John 2:4). When Jesus was asked by His brothers to go up to Jerusalem, He said, **My time has not yet come** (John 7:6, 8). And no man could lay a hand on Him in the temple or in the treasury because **His hour had not yet come** (John 7:30, 8:20).

Now Jesus' hour had come (John 13:1). The time for which He came into the world was at hand. During the last night of His life Jesus gave His disciples some final instructions and reassured them of His love (chapters 13–17). Only John's gospel provides the rich details of Jesus' final night with His disciples.

Now, before you begin, please ask God to reveal Himself through His Word and to transform you into the image of His Son. May God bless your diligent study of God's Word.

1. John 13:1 says Jesus loved His own **to the end** (NIV 1984: "showed them the full extent of His love"). The Greek phrase (*eis telos*) can mean "to the end" (without cessation) or "to the utmost" (fully). Take a minute to think about Jesus' relationship with His disciples as it compares to your relationship to those you love (family, friends, etc.).

    a. Do you love others without ceasing as Jesus did, and

Volunteer Rule:

If the leader asks for volunteers to read, pray, and answer the questions, group members will be more inclined to invite newcomers.

ADD GROUP INSIGHTS BELOW

17

do you show them the full extent of your love, or is your love often conditional—a love based upon their actions or your emotions at the time?

_____

_____

_____

b. What specific things could you do to be more Christlike in your love for others?

_____

_____

_____

_____

2. The Bible says Satan put into Judas Iscariot's heart to betray Jesus (John 13:2). Later in the chapter the Bible says **Satan entered him** (John 13:27). These verses have led some to believe that Christians can be demon-possessed, and spiritual deliverance or exorcism is the only thing that will rid a believer of an evil spirit or demon.

a. Do you believe a nonbeliever can be demon-possessed? Why?

_____

_____

b. Do you believe a Christian can be demon-possessed (Ephesians 4:27; 2 Timothy 2:24–26)?

_____

_____

_____

3. After the evening meal (commonly known as the Last Supper) Jesus rose, took off His outer garments, girded Himself with

a towel, and washed the disciples' feet, including Judas's (John 13:4ff.). Jesus assumed the role of a household servant whose routine responsibilities included washing the dusty feet of honored guests when they entered the home of the host.

a. How did Peter initially respond to Jesus' desire to wash his feet (John 13:6–8)?

_____

_____

b. What did Jesus mean when He said, **If I do not wash you, you have no part with Me** (John 13:8)?

_____

_____

c. If Jesus' statement to Peter in John 13:10 refers to salvation, what do you think He meant when He said, **He who is bathed needs only to wash his feet, but is completely clean** (John 13:10; 1 John 1:9)?

_____

_____

_____

4. Some Christian churches believe Jesus' statements **you ought to wash one another's feet** (John 13:14) and **I have given you an example, that you should do as I have done to you** (John 13:15) are commands that the church should practice today. Others believe Jesus' command is fulfilled when believers humbly serve one another.

a. The word *hermeneutics* (pronounced *her-me-noo-tics*; from the Greek word *hermeneutikos*—"to interpret") is used to refer to *the study of the methodical principles of interpreting the Bible*. Do you think foot-washing should be practiced by Christians today? Why? Be careful not to dismiss this command simply because it doesn't seem convenient.

_____

_____

_____

_____

b. If you believe Jesus' act of foot-washing is an example for believers to serve others, how are you fulfilling Christ's command to humbly serve others in your family, at work, at church?

_____

_____

c. What promise did Jesus give everyone who obeys this important command (John 13:17)?

_____

_____

_____

5. Jesus' promises of spiritual cleansing (salvation) and blessing for obedience apply to only those who are redeemed. Only they receive the assurance of God's forgiveness and the hope of His blessing.

a. Judas walked with Christ and the other apostles for approximately three years. During that time he heard the message of salvation countless times, but he was never saved. Proximity to truth does not automatically mean possession of truth. Are you absolutely certain you have been redeemed according to God's Word? If not, please read "The Final Exam" at the end of this study. It will explain in full what it means to be saved or born again.

_____

_____

_____

b. If you are a Christian, are you always careful about what you say to nonbelievers so they don't get a false sense of spiritual security?

_____

_____

6. Jesus quoted from Psalm 41:9 when He revealed that one of the apostles would betray Him, But He didn't positively identify who it was (John 13:21). Peter motioned to a disciple who was lying next to Jesus (assumed to be John) to ask Him who was the betrayer (John 13:24). Jesus said it was the one to whom He would give the piece of bread, and then He gave the bread to Judas (John 13:26). Why do you think the apostles still didn't realize that Judas was the traitor (John 12:4–6, 13:27–30)?

_____

_____

_____

_____

_____

_____

_____

7. After Judas went out into the night Jesus informed the apostle that the time had come for the Son of Man to be glorified and God to be glorified in Him (John 13:31–32).

a. What new commandment did Jesus give the apostles (John 13:34)?

_____

_____

b. What amazing promise does Christ give every believer who loves other believers as Christ loves them (John 13:35)?

_____

_____

_____

_____

_____

c. Why it is so difficult for believers, who have been shown the unconditional love of God, to obey His command to love one another?

_____

_____

_____

8. Simon Peter proclaimed his loyalty to Jesus by stating that he was willing to follow Him anywhere—even to martyrdom (John 13:36–37). Jesus, however, was not impressed with Peter's declaration of loyalty and informed him that he would deny Him three times before the next morning (John 13:38 NIV: "before the rooster crows"). What important spiritual truth didn't Peter understand about following Christ at this time (Matthew 26:41; John 6:63)?

_____

_____

_____

_____

_____

THREE

JESUS IS THE WAY

Read John 14;
other references as given.

Jesus told the apostles He was going away and they couldn't follow Him then (John 13:33, 36). His words were unsettling to the apostles who loved their Lord and were aware of the Jews' plan to kill Jesus and maybe His followers as well.

In John 14 Jesus assures the eleven remaining apostles of His plan to return to take them to a place He would prepare for them (John 14:1–14, **My Father's house**). Jesus also promised to send another Helper, the Holy Spirit, to comfort and guide them to do even greater works than He did on earth (John 14:15–31).

Now, before you begin, please ask God to reveal Himself through His Word and to transform you into the image of His Son. May God bless your diligent study of God's Word.

Focus Rule:

If the leader helps the group members focus on the Bible, they will gain confidence to study God's Word on their own.

———

ADD GROUP
INSIGHTS BELOW

1. While Jesus and His disciples are still in the Upper Room, what two promises did He give to comfort them (John 14:1–3)?

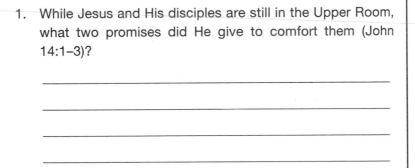

2. The apostle Thomas is commonly known as *Doubting Thomas*. Thomas's inquiry about Jesus' destination and how to get there, however, seems to be a refreshing example of uninhibited spiritual interest and should motivate many to find answers to their unvoiced spiritual questions.

    a. What did Jesus tell Thomas about where He was going and how to get there (John 14:6)?

    _____

    _____

    _____

    _____

    b. Thomas asked Jesus where He was going and how he could know the way. If you had had an opportunity to answer Thomas's question, what would you have said?

    _____

    _____

    _____

3. Jesus' answer to Thomas is clear and comprehensive. Absolutely no one can come to the Father except through Jesus Christ (John 14:6). To many people, even those who claim to be Christians, Jesus' statement seems narrow and even bigoted.

    a. Do you believe there are other ways to God than trusting completely in Jesus Christ? Why?

    _____

    _____

    b. What did the apostle Peter teach about Jesus being the only way to God (Acts 4:12)?

    _____

_____

_____

Drawing Rule:

To learn how to draw everyone into the group discussion without calling on anyone, go to www.Lamplighters USA.org/training.

———

ADDITIONAL INSIGHTS

c. What did the apostle Paul teach about Jesus being the only way to God (Acts 17:29–31)?

_____

_____

_____

d. What did Paul say to the Galatian churches to warn them about the teachers who taught a different way to heaven—a different gospel other than through faith in Jesus Christ alone (Galatians 1:8–9)?

_____

_____

_____

4. Name at least four important truths Jesus taught Thomas and Philip about His relationship with God the Father (John 14:7–11)?

_____

_____

_____

_____

_____

5. Jesus said that everyone who believes (completely trusts) in Him will do greater works than He did. How can this be (John 14:12–14)?

_____

_____

_____

_____

_____

_____

6. John 14:15 is an interesting verse because it can be translated two different ways from the Greek language: (1) **If you love Me, keep My commandments** (KJV, NKJV) and (2) **If you love Me, you will keep My commandments** (NASB, ESV). While both renderings are accurate, they convey two completely different meanings. Explain how these two legitimate translations differ.

_____

_____

_____

_____

7. Jesus said He would pray that the Father who would send another **Helper** (NIV 1984: "Counselor") or the **Spirit of truth** (John 14:16–17).

   a. Who is this Helper or Counselor (John 14:16–17, 26)?

   _____

   b. Even though Jesus presented detailed instruction on the person and ministry of the Holy Spirit in John 16:7–15, He taught some important truths about the Holy Spirit in John 14:16–17, 26. Please name at least five facts about the Holy Spirit and His ministry (John 14:16–17, 26).

   _____

   _____

   _____

   _____

_____

_____

8. Some religious groups believe the Holy Spirit is not really God, but only a force or agent of God. How do we know that the Holy Spirit is truly God and not merely an attribute of God or extension of Him (John 14:16–17; Acts 5:1-4, Hebrews 9:14)?

_____

_____

_____

_____

9. a. John 14:21 teaches some important truths about a believer's spiritual growth. List at least three.

_____

_____

_____

_____

   b. The writer of Hebrews rebuked the believers for not making steady spiritual progress (Hebrews 5:12–14). He said they had come **to need milk and not solid food** (Hebrews 5:11–12). What did the writer mean when he used this metaphor?

_____

_____

_____

10. Jesus promised to leave the apostles with a peace that is different than the world's version of peace (John 14:27). In what ways do you think the peace of God is different from the world's concept of peace?

Has your group become a "Holy huddle?" Learn how to reach out to others by taking online leadership training.

_____

ADDITIONAL INSIGHTS

_____

_____

_____

_____

11. Jesus said **I will no longer talk much with you, for the ruler of this world is coming, and he has nothing in Me** (John 14:30).

   a. What do you think Jesus meant when He said, **the ruler of this world is coming?**

   _____

   _____

   _____

   b. What did Jesus mean when He said, **he has nothing in Me** (John 14:30)?

   _____

   _____

   _____

   _____

   c. Does the ruler of this world have anything in you? If so, what should you do so you can say, like Jesus, that **he has nothing in Me** (1 John 1:9)?

   _____

   _____

   _____

   _____

FOUR

THE TRUE VINE

Read John 15;
other references as given.

Throughout the Old Testament (OT hereafter) Israel is pictured as a choice vine/vineyard (Psalm 80:8; Isaiah 5:1–7; Jeremiah 2:21, 6:9; Ezekiel 15; Hosea 10:1, 14:7) and God as its vinedresser or gardener. God tenderly cared for His vine (Israel) and anticipated choice fruit (righteousness, justice, holiness), but He often received only wild and worthless grapes (wickedness, oppression, idolatry, etc.).

In John 15 Jesus identifies Himself as the *true vine* and genuine believers as (living) branches that bear **fruit** and **more fruit** (John 15:2) and **much fruit** (John 15:5, 8)—if they abide in Him. Jesus explains how His followers can abide in Him (John 15:1–8), how they can fulfill His previous commandment to love one another (John 15:9–17), and how believers can live righteously in a world that hates the One they love (John 15:18–27).

Now, before you begin, please ask God to reveal Himself through His Word and to transform you into the image of His Son. May God bless your diligent study of God's Word.

Gospel Gold
Rule:

Try to get all the answers to the questions—not just the easy ones. Go for the gold.

ADD GROUP
INSIGHTS BELOW

1. The illustration of a vinedresser and his vineyard is a powerful illustration that no Israelite would have misunderstood. Everyone knew how hard a vinedresser worked, how carefully he handled the vines, and the disappointment he experienced when the vines failed to produce good grapes.

a. In the illustration of God and His vine, what all did God do to help Israel produce good fruit (Isaiah 5:1– 2)?

_____

_____

_____

_____

b. What did God do to His vineyard (Israel) when the nation consistently failed to produce good fruit (Isaiah 5:3–6)?

_____

_____

_____

_____

2. In John 15:1–8 Jesus recalls the familiar OT image of the vinedresser and the vine to teach a powerful spiritual truth. Followers of Christ must learn to **abide** (Greek *meno*: to abide, to remain) in Him if they expect to bear much fruit (John 15:4–7). The frequent use of word **abide** (11 times in John 15 and 40 times in John's gospel) emphasizes this fact.

a. The vinedresser cuts off the dead branches and burns them in the fire (John 15:2, 6). The living branches (believers—those who produce any fruit whatsoever) are pruned so they will bear more fruit (John 15:2). How does God *prune* a Christian so that he bears more fruit (Hebrews 12:9–11)?

_____

_____

b. Give an example of how God has used adversity to bring about more godliness in your life. Perhaps you could describe how God has used adversity to bring you to salvation.

_____

_____

_____

Balance Rule:

To learn how to balance the group discussion, go to www.Lamplighters USA.org/training.

_____

ADDITIONAL INSIGHTS

3. In Hebrew 12:11 the phrase **the peaceable fruit of righteousness** (NIV: "harvest of righteousness") may seem rather ambiguous or obscure, but the apostle Paul describes this fruit more clearly.

    a. List the nine fruits of the Spirit that God wants to manifest in your life (Galatians 5:22–23).

    _____

    _____

    _____

    b. If the evidence of abiding in Christ is the fruit of the Spirit, would those who know you best say that you have learned to abide in Christ?

    _____

    _____

    _____

4. With Christ's crucifixion less than 24 hours away, Jesus continued to prepare the apostles for a new relationship with Him. No longer would they have His physical presence with them. _They must learn how to abide in Christ._

    a. What do you think it means to **abide in Christ** (John 15:4–5)?

    _____

    _____

    b. What are four results of abiding in Christ (John 15:5, 7, 9–11)?

_____

_____

_____

_____

5. John 15:12–16 is an interesting passage because Jesus makes a distinction between the disciples being His friends and His servants. It was the normal practice for a disciple to choose a teacher to follow. Jesus reversed that order and said the apostles had not chosen Him, but He had chosen them (John 15:16). Furthermore, Jesus wasn't diminishing the concept of the master-slave relationship that Paul uses so generously in several of his writings (Romans 1:1; Philippians 1:1).

    a. Jesus Christ commands Christians to love one another (John 15:12). To what extent are believers to fulfill this command (John 15:12–13; 1 Peter 1:22)?

        _____

        _____

        _____

    b. Give at least two reasons why the apostles could be considered Jesus' friends rather than merely His servants (John 15:12–16).

        _____

        _____

        _____

        _____

6. Jesus told His disciples to not be troubled even though He was leaving them (John 14:1, 3). He would love them even after He left (John 14:19–21) and would send the Holy Spirit to comfort and guide them (John 16:7). If they learned to

abide in Christ, they could accomplish even greater things than He did when He was on earth (John 14:12).

a. If the disciples followed Jesus and obeyed His teachings, the world would hate them (John 15:18–16:4). The Greek word (*kosmos*) is used variously in Scripture, and students of the Bible must study the immediate context to determine its specific meaning. Who or what do you think is meant by the phrase **the world** in John 15:18–25)? Be as definitive as possible with your answer.

_____

_____

_____

b. Do you think it is possible for a Christian to be **of the world**? Why?

_____

_____

_____

Did you know Lamplighters is more than a small group ministry? It is a discipleship training ministry that uses a small group format to train disciple-makers. If every group trained one person per study, God would use these new disciple-makers to reach more people for Christ.

ADDITIONAL INSIGHTS

7. Some Christians believe the term *worldly Christian* is an oxymoron (a combination of contradictory or incongruous terms such as "a cruel kindness"). The apostle Paul, however, chastened the Corinthian believers because they were behaving carnally or worldly (1 Corinthians 3:1–3). If you are a Christian, take a minute to honestly evaluate yourself. In what of the following areas of your life are you exhibiting evidences of worldliness or carnality? Circle the words.

Anger/Temper	Unforgiveness	Lust
Revenge	Gossip/Slander	Backbiting
Boasting	Immorality	Occult
Jealousy	Drunkenness	Envy
Hatred	Lying	Greed
Materialism	Yelling	Malice/Ill-will
Hypocrisy	Spiritual Apathy	
Non-Pres. Drugs	(including tobacco)	

8. List four reasons why faithful followers of Jesus Christ should expect persecution in this world (John 15:19–25).

_____

_____

_____

_____

_____

_____

_____

_____

9. The church often struggles with knowing how to live in a world that hates Jesus and is hostile to His true followers. Some have withdrawn themselves physically from society, but this leads to a failure to fulfill Christ's command to make disciples (Matthew 28:18–20). Others have befriended the world and compromised their loyalty to Christ. What does the Bible teach regarding the proper balance for the believer who is in the world but not of the world, so he can fulfill Jesus' command to rescue those who still are of the world (Philippians 2:14–16)?

_____

_____

_____

_____

_____

FIVE

THE HOLY SPIRIT

Read John 16; other references as given.

In John 15 Jesus taught His disciples the need to abide in Him, the true vine. If they learned to abide in Him, they would bear fruit, more fruit, and much fruit. But if the disciples failed to abide in Him they would not bear fruit because, without Him, they could do nothing (John 15:5).

In John 16 Jesus continued to warn the apostles about the persecution they would face after His death (John 16:1–4). Then He taught the disciples about the ministry of the Holy Spirit (John 16:5–15) and explained how their sorrow would eventually be turned to joy when they fully understood God's plan of redemption (John 16:16–33).

Now, before you begin, please ask God to reveal Himself through His Word and to transform you into the image of His Son. May God bless your diligent study of God's Word.

No-Trespassing Rule:

To keep the Bible study on track, avoid talking about political parties, church denominations, and Bible translations.

ADD GROUP INSIGHTS BELOW

1. a. What did Jesus tell the apostles would happen if they continued to follow His ways (John 16:1–3)?

    _____

    _____

    _____

    b. Why have Christians continued to be persecuted throughout the history of the church (John 16:3; 1 Corinthians 2:14)?

_____

_____

_____

2. The words **But now** indicate the time was soon approaching for Jesus to be separated from His disciples. Only a few more instructions would be given to the disciples before He left the Upper Room for the garden of Gethsemane where He was arrested (John 16:5–17:26).

    a. Jesus said it was beneficial for Him to leave because He would send the Holy Spirit (John 16:7). What do the following verses teach about the person and work of the Holy Spirit (John 16:7–15)?

    _____

    _____

    _____

    _____

    _____

    _____

    _____

    _____

    b. What role does the Holy Spirit play in man's salvation (John 16:8–11; Titus 3:5–6)?

    _____

    _____

    _____

    _____

    _____

c. The Holy Spirit **will convict the world of sin** (John 16:8). Who or what is meant by **the world** (John 16:8, 15:18–19)?

_____

_____

3. Some Christians marginalize the Holy Spirit's person and work, and others overemphasize it. John 16:13–15 is a key passage that helps believers understand the Third Person of the Trinity and His ministry. What important truths are taught in this passage about the Holy Spirit (John 16:13–15)?

_____

_____

_____

_____

4. a. A Christian must learn to follow the leading of the Holy Spirit if he expects to abide in Christ and bear much fruit. List two things a believer must *not* do if he expects to abide in Christ (Ephesians 4:30; 1 Thessalonians 5:19)?

_____

_____

_____

_____

b. What do you think is the difference between grieving the Holy Spirit and quenching the Holy Spirit?

_____

_____

_____

5. Many believers are confused about the meaning of the two phrases, *being baptized in the (Holy) Spirit* and *being filled with the (Holy) Spirit.*

a. What does it mean to be baptized by the Spirit (1 Corinthians 12:12-13; Titus 3:5)?

_____

_____

_____

Have you been baptized in the Spirit? When did this happen?

_____

_____

b. Believers are never commanded to be baptized in the Spirit, but they are commanded **to be filled with the Spirit** (Ephesians 5:18). What do you think this means (Ephesians 5:18)?

_____

_____

6. Jesus said, **A little while, and you will not see Me; and again a little while, and you will see Me, because I go to the Father** (John 16:16), but the apostles didn't understand what He meant (John 16:17). Did Jesus mean (1) He would return in the person of the Spirit (a view supported by the immediate context), (2) He would return eventually after He had prepared a place for them in heaven (a view supported by Jesus' comment in John 14:1–4), or (3) He would see them after He was resurrected before He ascended to the Father? Look closely at the apostles' question (John 16:18) and Jesus' answer (John 16:19–22). Which of these three possible interpretations do you think is the best interpretation of Jesus' words in John 16:16? Be prepared to support your answer.

_____

_____

_____

_____

_____

7. Jesus prepared the apostles for a new relationship with Him through the abiding presence of the Holy Spirit. They would be grieved over His death, but their sorrow would turn to joy when they understood the resurrection. But like Jesus, they would suffer persecution (John 15:18–16:4).

    a. Beside the abiding ministry of the Holy Spirit, what else did Jesus promise the disciples to help them overcome the trials they would face after His departure (John 16:23–24)?

    _____

    _____

    _____

    b. Do you experience fullness of joy as a result of your prayers being answered?

    _____

    _____

    _____

    _____

8. When the disciples asked Jesus to teach them to pray, He instructed them to pray directly to the Father (Matthew 6:5–15; Luke 11:2–4) and to pray **in My [Jesus']** name (John 16:23–24). If praying in Jesus' name is not a magical formula that's added at the end of a prayer to guarantee its success, what do you think it means to pray **in Jesus' name**?

    _____

    _____

9. Jesus' teaching about His imminent death was unsettling to the apostles, who didn't fully understand the resurrection.

Jesus promised them peace in the midst of coming tribulation (John 16:33).

a. Jesus said He had **overcome the world** (John 16:33). How does a believer overcome the world (1 John 5:4)?

_____

_____

b. If you are a Christian, are you overcoming the world by progressively living by faith, or are you living in spiritual defeat because you haven't surrendered one or more areas of your life to God?

_____

_____

_____

_____

Six

What Would Jesus Pray?

**Read John 17;
other references as given.**

Jesus' formal training of the apostles was complete. He had given them all the words that the Father had given Him (John 17:4, 8).

John 17 is the only record of the greatest prayer ever offered. This prayer, often known as Jesus' High Priestly Prayer or the Lord's Prayer (not to be confused with the Lord's prayer in Matthew 6:9–13), was likely prayed in the Upper Room or as Jesus walked with His disciples to the garden of Gethsemane. Jesus prayed for Himself (John 17:1–5), the apostles (John 17:6–19), and for all future believers (John 17:20–26). His prayer allows us to understand how passionately Jesus loved His followers.

Now, before you begin, please ask God to reveal Himself through His Word and to transform you into the image of His Son. May God bless your diligent study of God's Word.

Transformation
Rule:

Seek for personal
transformation,
not mere
information, from
God's Word.

———

ADD GROUP
INSIGHTS BELOW

1. Many Christians have been taught the helpful acronym ACTS as a model for praying: *adoration*—a time to praise God and magnify His name; *confession*—a time to confess sin; thanksgiving—a time to thank God for His goodness and gifts; *supplication*—a time to ask God for the needs in our lives.

    a. What do you notice about Jesus' prayer that is different than the ACTS model of praying (John 17:1–5)?

_____

_____

_____

_____

   b. What can you learn from Christ's prayer that you can use when you pray?

_____

_____

_____

_____

2. When Jesus said **Father ... glorify Your Son, that Your Son also may glorify You** (John 17:1), He was asking the Father to reveal the true person, presence, and power of Jesus as the Christ during His coming death so He (Jesus), in turn, might reveal the true person, presence, and power of the Father.

   a. What was the ultimate goal of Christ's death on the cross (John 17:2)?

_____

_____

   b. What is the definition of eternal life (John 17:3)?

_____

_____

_____

3. Everything Jesus did during His incarnation (His earthly existence) was for the glory of God the Father (John 17:4). He was never confused about who He was or His life purpose. The unsaved don't know God so they can't understand God or their true life purpose. Many Christians are also confused

about who they are in relationship to God and their purpose for living.

a.   If you are a Christian, what should be the goal of your life including everything you say and do (Romans 16:27; 1 Corinthians 10:31)?

_____

_____

b.   A believer glorifies God when his actions and words, including the thoughts and meditations of his heart, bring honor and praise to God and inspire others to do the same. Can you honestly say that God's glory is your ultimate life goal, or are you confused about why you are alive and why God saved you?

_____

_____

_____

4.   What did Jesus pray to be restored to Him (John 17:5)? Why was it missing (Philippians 2:5–11)?

_____

_____

_____

5.   Jesus revealed the Father's true nature to everyone the Father had given Him out of the world (John 17:6). What else did Jesus desire His followers to know (John 17:7,10)?

_____

_____

_____

6.   Jesus asked the Father to **keep through Your name those whom You have given Me** (John 17:11). Then Jesus said

Would you like to learn how to prepare a life-changing Bible study using a simple 4-step process? Contact Lamplighters and ask about ST-A-R-T.

ADDITIONAL INSIGHTS

He had **kept them in Your name** (John 17:12).

a. These two statements are similar. List three specific things Jesus wanted the Father to do for His followers (John 17:12–18).

_____

_____

_____

b. Judas is the **son of perdition** (utter destruction, damnation, hell) who was lost (John 17:12). Can a true believer ever be lost (John 17:12; 10:28–29)? Why?

_____

_____

_____

7. Like a good shepherd Jesus was concerned for His sheep after His departure because the world would hate them (John 17:14).

a. What did Jesus ask the Father to do to protect His followers from the world (John 17:15–17)?

_____

_____

_____

b. What did Jesus say He would do to help His followers stay faithful to God (John 17:19)?

_____

_____

_____

8. Jesus didn't want His followers to be taken out of the world (John 17:15), but He wanted them to be kept from Satan's

power (the evil one). Jesus prayed for His followers to be sent into the world in the same way the Father sent Him (John 17:18).

a. What does Jesus send His followers into the world to do (Matthew 28:18–20; Acts 1:8)?

_____

_____

b. Jesus prayed that His followers would (1) be in the world but not of the world (John 17:15–16), (2) be protected from the evil one (John 17:15), and (3) be effective witnesses for Him (John 17:18). What do you think must happen for all these things to occur?

_____

_____

9. In John 17:20 Jesus began the third section of His prayer. He prayed for all future believers of all ethnic backgrounds, including us. What is Jesus' initial request for them (John 17:20–23)?

_____

_____

_____

_____

_____

10. John 17:21 is a favorite verse for promoters of the modern ecumenical movement. The ecumenical movement is a worldwide endeavor to bring spiritual oneness to the entire Christian (evangelical and liberal) church, then to the entire religious world (including Hindu, Muslim, etc.), through confession, reconciliation, and a commitment to a one-world church. According to the leaders of the ecumenical movement, doctrinal differences and specific

If the leader places a watch on the table, participants will feel confident that the Bible study will be completed on time. If the leader doesn't complete the lesson each week, participants will be less likely to do their weekly lessons, and the discussion will not be as rich.

ADDITIONAL INSIGHTS

religious beliefs should be surrendered for the greater goal of spiritual oneness.

a. What is the basis for true spiritual unity among all believers (John 17:21, 23–24)?

_____

_____

b. What is the difference between unity and unanimity? Use a dictionary if you like.

_____

_____

_____

_____

11. Evangelicals generally regard the modern ecumenical movement as fundamentally flawed and unscriptural. On the other hand, many believers are factious in spirit and unloving and violate Christ's command to love one another (John 13:34–35). What do you think a believer should do to fulfill Christ's command to love other members of the body of Christ but not compromise the truth?

_____

_____

_____

_____

_____

SEVEN

BETRAYAL IN THE GARDEN

> ## Read John 18;
> ## other references as given.

In John 17 Jesus prayed for His disciples and all future believers. Then He left the Upper Room and led His disciples across the Kidron Valley to the garden of Gethsemane. The garden (actually a small olive tree orchard) is located on the western slope of the Mount of Olives about one half mile from the eastern wall of the old city of Jerusalem. Jesus and His disciples stayed on the Mount of Olives every night during the Passover week (Luke 21:37), likely using the garden area as a bivouac (temporary overnight lodging) and a place of prayer and solitude (cf. John 18:2).

In John 18 Jesus is arrested by a detachment of Roman soldiers led by Judas. He is brought before Annas (John 18:12–23), Caiaphas (John 18:24–27), and Pontius Pilate (John 18:28–40). In this lesson you will learn how God even uses the wickedness of man to accomplish His divine will.

Now, before you begin, please ask God to reveal Himself through His Word and to transform you into the image of His Son. May God bless your diligent study of God's Word.

If the leader asks all the study questions, the group discussion will be more likely to stay on track.

ADD GROUP INSIGHTS BELOW

1. While Jesus was giving His final instructions to the disciples (John 13:31–16:33) and offering His high priestly prayer (John 17), Judas was making plans with the Jewish leaders and Roman officials to capture Jesus.

   a. What happened when Judas, the Roman soldiers, and

officers from the chief priests and Pharisees came into the garden with their lanterns, torches, and weapons (John 18:4)?

_____

_____

_____

b. Jesus told those who were looking for Him **I am He**. (John 18:5). What happened next (John 18:6)?

_____

_____

_____

c. Why do you think this happened when Jesus said, **I am He**?

_____

_____

_____

2. Jesus' response to those who came to arrest Him is very intriguing (John 18:5–6, 8). In the Greek New Testament, Jesus responded with the words **I am** when He identified Himself as Jesus of Nazareth (John 18:5–6, 8). Several English translations add the word *He* at the end of Jesus' statement to complete the thought, but other translations (NKJV, NASB) italicize the word *He* to indicate that it was not in the original Greek text. Some Bible scholars see Jesus' simple statement **I am** as an overt claim to His deity.

a. What did God tell Moses to say about who had sent him to deliver the Israelites out of the hand of Pharaoh in Egypt (Exodus 3:14)?

_____

_____

b. What did Jesus tell the Jews when they questioned Him about His relationship to the patriarch Abraham (John 8:58)?

_____

c. How did the Jews understand Jesus' statement in John 8:58 (John 8:59; Leviticus 24:16)?

_____

_____

_____

_____

The Bible says, *So then faith comes by hearing and hearing by the word of God* (Romans 10:17). Every time you humbly study God's Word, your faith grows.

———

ADDITIONAL INSIGHTS

3. a. Jesus used the words **I AM** several times throughout the book of John. List the seven **I AM** statements made by Jesus (John 6:35; 8:12; 10:7; 10:11; 11:25; 14:6; 15:1).

_____

_____

_____

_____

_____

_____

_____

b. The words translated **I AM** were so revered among the Jews that no Jewish person would consciously utter the words because they had been used by God to identify Himself. What do you think Jesus was communicating to His listeners (and us, as well) when He repeatedly used these sacred words?

_____

_____

_____

_____

_____

4. In John 18:1–11 there is a striking contrast of characters. Among the captors Judas was motivated by greed, the Jewish leaders by a love for power and desire to control the people, and the Roman soldiers by duty and a concern over social unrest and a possible insurrection.

    a. How did Peter respond during this confrontation (John 18:10)?

    _____

    _____

    b. What did Jesus do in response to Peter's aggressive action (John 18:11; Luke 22:50–51)?

    _____

    _____

    _____

    c. Do you normally respond like Peter at a time of crisis (at home, work, church, etc.), or do you respond like Jesus who often brought peace, comfort, and healing to times of crisis?

    _____

    _____

    _____

    _____

    _____

5. Jesus was arrested and led to Annas, the father-in-law of the high priest Caiaphas (John 18:13). Annas had been high priest from AD 6 to 15, but he had been deposed by Pontius Pilate's predecessor Valerus Gratus. Although five of his

sons and his son-in-law (Caiaphas) served as high priests, many scholars believe Annas was still the real religious power behind the scenes.

It's a good time to begin praying and inviting new people for your next Open House.

ADDITIONAL INSIGHTS

a. What noteworthy event happened while Jesus was being interrogated by Annas and Caiaphas (John 18:16–17, 25–27)?

_____

_____

_____

b. What happened when Peter realized that he had denied the Lord three times exactly as Jesus had prophesied (Luke 22:59–62)?

_____

c. Have you ever denied allegiance to Jesus Christ, either directly or by your silence, because you were fearful or ashamed to be identified as one of His followers? If so, what were the circumstances?

_____

_____

_____

_____

_____

6. Jesus faced two preliminary hearings and four trials prior to His crucifixion—of which three were religious and three were civil. Jesus was interrogated sequentially by (1) Annas (John 18:12–23), (2) Caiaphas (John 18:24–27; Matthew 26:57–67), (3) the Sanhedrin (Matthew 27:1–2), (4) Pilate (John 18:28–38), (5) Herod (Luke 23:6–12), and (6) Pilate (John 18:39–19:16). Caiaphas sent Jesus to the Praetorium (NIV: "palace") where He was questioned by Pontius Pilate (trial #2) who was the Roman prefect or governor of Judea

(AD 26–36). The Judean governor lived in Caesarea, but he routinely came to Jerusalem during the three Pilgrim Feasts in the event of a riot or other civil disturbance.

a. The Jews accused Jesus of (1) attempting to pervert or subvert the Roman nation, (2) refusing to pay taxes to Caesar, and (3) claiming to be a king in opposition to Caesar (Luke 23:1–2). Why do you think they brought these three specific accusations before Pilate when their real problem with Jesus was His claim to be the Christ (John 18:28–32, 38)?

_____

_____

_____

_____

_____

b. The Jews wanted Jesus to be crucified by the Romans rather than stoning Him themselves. They believed anyone who was crucified was cursed by God (Deuteronomy 21:23). If Jesus was crucified, God would curse Him, and the Jewish people would turn away from Him. Rather than becoming a curse, what unique thing happened as a result of Jesus' death on a cross (Galatians 3:13)?

_____

_____

_____

7. During Jesus' first appearance before Pilate, the governor wasn't convinced that He had done anything worthy of the death penalty (John 18:38). What do you think Jesus meant by the statement **My kingdom is not of this world** (John 18:36)?

_____

_____

_____

_____

_____

_____

8. Jesus is the great (eternal) King who will reign on earth during the millennial kingdom in the future. Now He is gathering citizens (through salvation) who are citizens of His future kingdom (Philippians 3:20). If you are a Christian and a citizen of heaven, what is your present role and responsibility to your King and His coming kingdom (2 Corinthians 5:20–21)?

_____

_____

_____

ADDITIONAL INSIGHTS

Eight

It Is Finished

Read John 19;
other references as given.

In John 18 Jesus appeared before Annas, Caiaphas, and Pilate. Pilate wasn't convinced Jesus was guilty and sent Him to King Herod (Luke 23:6–12). Initially Herod was delighted to meet Jesus, but he became offended when Jesus refused to answer his questions and mocked Him by placing an elegant purple robe on Him. This obvious insult was aimed at Jesus' claim to be a king and clear evidence that Herod didn't understand His true identity.

In John 19 Jesus was returned to Pilate where He was condemned to die (John 18:39–19:16), crucified (John 19:17–37), and buried (John 19:38–42). In this lesson you'll learn how the Jews were able to manipulate Pilate into crucifying Jesus and what Jesus meant when He uttered the words **It is finished** (John 19:30).

Now, before you begin, please ask God to reveal Himself through His Word and to transform you into the image of His Son. May God bless your diligent study of God's Word.

1. What five things did the Roman soldiers do to Jesus during His second trial before Pilate (John 19:1–3)?

    _____

    _____

    _____

Is your study going well? Consider starting a new group. To learn how, go to www. Lamplighters USA.org/training.

———

ADD GROUP INSIGHTS BELOW

_____

_____

2. Many people say that Jesus is not God, but merely a good moral teacher like Confucius and Buddha, or a prophet like Mohammed. But this cannot be true! If Jesus is only a good moral teacher or a prophet, then He lied to the people by telling them He was God (John 10:30; 3:13–14). Since a fundamental characteristic of good teachers is that they don't lie to their students, Jesus' unwillingness to recant His claim to deity leaves only three possibilities: (1) He is a liar; (2) He is a lunatic—someone who actually thought He was God but was not; or (3) He is Lord – exactly who He claimed to be.

a. Who did the Jewish leaders believe Jesus to be (John 19:7; 10:31–33)?

_____

b. Who did Pilate believe Jesus to be (John 19:9–10)?

_____

_____

c. Who do you believe Jesus is?

_____

_____

What does that mean to you?

_____

_____

_____

3. Why was Pilate afraid when he heard the statement **He made Himself the Son of God** (John 19:7–8; Matthew 27:19)?

_____

_____

_____

It's time to choose your next study. Turn to the back of the study guide for a list of available studies or go online for the latest studies.

_____

ADDITIONAL INSIGHTS

4. a. The last two words of Jesus' statement **You could have no power at all against Me unless it had been given you from above** are interesting (John 19:11). A reader might be inclined to think it should read _from below_ (referring to the demonic powers at work at that time). What do you think Jesus meant when He made this significant spiritual statement?

_____

_____

_____

_____

   b. Pilate had the authority to order Jesus' crucifixion. According to John 19:11, Jesus said it was God who gave Pilate the power to do evil against Jesus. Do you think God gives men power to do evil (John 19:11; Habakkuk 1:5–11)? If so, does this make God the author of sin? Why?

_____

_____

_____

_____

5. The Jewish leaders were desperately looking for a way to convince Pilate to crucify Jesus. The Jews hated Pilate for his harsh leadership and some blatant acts of incompetence, including having his soldiers parade through the streets with an image of the Roman emperor on a Jewish holy day. His harsh leadership and actions had so infuriated the Jews that they sent a delegation to Rome to complain about

him. The Roman emperor Tiberius was well-known for his suspicious nature and particularly alert to any form of rebellion throughout the Roman Empire.

a. What did the Jewish leaders say to Pilate that triggered his own insecurities and sealed Jesus' fate (John 19:12–13)?

_____

_____

_____

b. What statement did the Jews make that revealed their spiritual bankruptcy?

_____

_____

6. It has been said that the Romans did not invent crucifixion, but they perfected it. Crucifixion was designed to cause an excruciatingly slow death with the victim ultimately dying of asphyxiation. The victim's hands and feet were nailed to a rough wooden cross where he hung writhing in unimaginable agony. Alternately, he supported himself by pushing on his feet or pulling his body up on his hands. When the victim supported his entire weight by his outstretched arms and his feet, it did little to alleviate his intense suffering or lessen the searing pain within his slowly collapsing lungs. And since Jesus had just been scourged, His open flesh wounds would have also pressed against the rough wooden cross as he moved up and down, increasing his pain and likely sending large slivers deep into his lacerated back.

a. Jesus endured the unfathomable agony of crucifixion for six long hours (Mark 15:25, 34–37). What else did Jesus endure on the cross (Luke 23:35–36, 39; Hebrews 12:2)?

_____

_____

_____

_____

b. Since Jesus was innocent of all charges against Him and he could have escaped, why did He subject Himself to such intense suffering (Colossians 2:13–14)?

_____

_____

_____

c. Does that include you? _____
Have you accepted Jesus' sacrificial death on the cross so that your sins and trespasses are forgiven forever?

_____

_____

7. Jesus made seven statements while He hung on the cross, including His second-to-last words on the cross, **It is finished** (John 19:30). Bible scholars have debated about the exact meaning of Jesus' final words. Do you think Jesus meant (1) His life was finished, (2) His ministry was finished, or (3) His work of redemption was complete?

_____

_____

_____

_____

_____

8. Two thieves were crucified with Jesus. Together the three of them could easily represent all humanity. Jesus is the only sinless Son of God; the first thief represents unbelieving humanity that rejects Jesus until its final hour (Luke 23:39); the second thief represents repentant humanity (Luke 23:40–42).

List three things the second thief said that indicated he was genuinely saved and not just making a superficial deathbed decision (Luke 23:40–42)?

_____

_____

_____

9. Several Old Testament prophecies were fulfilled by Jesus' trial and crucifixion. Match the statement below with the correct Old Testament prophecy by drawing a line that connects the correct answer.

a. Jesus was silent before Herod and Pilate	Psalm 34:20
b. None of Jesus' bones were broken	Psalm 22:16
c. The Roman soldiers cast lots for Jesus' clothes	Zechariah 12:10
d. Jesus' side was pierced	Isaiah 53:7
e. Jesus' hands and feet were pierced	Psalm 22:18

NINE

HE IS RISEN!

**Read John 20;
other references as given.**

Jesus was dead—or is He? The Jews thought the blasphemer was dead. The Romans thought the insurrectionist who claimed to be a king was dead. Even the disciples thought Jesus dead. But none of them understood the Old Testament prophecies about the resurrection or comprehended the power of God to raise Jesus from the grave.

John 19 is about death and defeat, but John 20 is about life and victory. Jesus is alive! He was raised from the grave by the power of God and appeared to Mary Magdalene and the disciples. In this lesson you'll learn God carefully orchestrated Christ's resurrection so that nobody could seriously believe His body was stolen.

Now, before you begin, please ask God to reveal Himself through His Word and to transform you into the image of His Son. May God bless your diligent study of God's Word.

Many groups study the Final Exam the week after the final lesson for three reasons: (1) someone might come to Christ, (2) believers gain assurance of salvation, (3) group members learn how to share the gospel.

———

ADD GROUP INSIGHTS BELOW

1. Mary Magdalene (Mary from Magdala or Magadan, a port town on the Sea of Galilee) came to Jesus' tomb early Sunday morning (the first day of the week). Note: This is not the same Mary who anointed Jesus' feet (John 12:3).

   a. What did Mary initially think had happened (John 20:1–2)?

   _____

   _____

b. What did she say to Jesus, who she assumed was the gardener (John 20:14–15)?

_____

_____

_____

2. Mary's reaction to the empty tomb is evidence of the spiritual confusion surrounding the events of Jesus' resurrection and an example of how a person's wrong thinking can cause unnecessary emotional pain. Now recall a situation in your life where your erroneous thinking (an unfounded suspicion, irrational reasoning, etc.) led you to a wrong conclusion and caused you (and perhaps others) unwarranted emotional pain. What should you do the next time you struggle with errant thoughts (2 Corinthians 10:4–5)?

_____

_____

_____

_____

3. a. Why do you think the disciples, including the women, had a hard time understanding the concept of the resurrection, especially when Jesus had repeatedly predicted his own resurrection (John 2:19; 14:3; 16:17), and they knew Jesus had raised Lazarus from the dead (John 3:27; 20:9)?

_____

_____

_____

b. List three things that should be present in a believer's life if he expects to consistently receive spiritual truth from God (John 14:21, James 4:6)?

_____

_____

_____

4. Mary assumed Jesus' body had been stolen (John 20:2, 15). When the Roman soldiers who guarded the tomb realized Jesus' body had disappeared, they went to the Jewish leaders, who gave them a large sum of money to say His body was stolen (Matthew 28:11–15). What evidence was left at the "crime scene" that indicates Jesus' body wasn't stolen as many believed (John 20:5–7)?

_____

_____

_____

_____

_____

5. Jesus revealed Himself to Mary (John 20:16). Why didn't Jesus want Mary to cling to him (John 20:17)?

_____

_____

Why do you think Jesus said this to Mary?

_____

_____

_____

6. Jesus' statement **As the Father has sent Me, I also send you** (John 20:21) is considered one of the five New Testament references that comprise the Great Commission (see also Matthew 28:18–20; Mark 16:15, Luke 24:46–49; Acts 1:8). The Great Commission is Jesus' commission or command to the church through the apostles to continue His work after His earthly ministry ceased.

Having trouble with your group? A Lamplighters trainer can help you solve the problem.

ADDITIONAL INSIGHTS

a. The church as a whole is often confused about the true gospel of Jesus Christ. To some the gospel is God's promise of health and wealth. To others it is the promise of a successful and wonderful life. Christians must understand the true definition of the gospel if they expect to fulfill Christ's command to make disciples of all nations (Matthew 28:19). Examine these two Great Commission verses to determine the biblical definition of the gospel (Mark 16:15; Luke 24:46–49).

_____

_____

_____

_____

b. Jesus commanded His followers to **Make disciples of all the nations** (Matthew 28:19). The extent of His command (of all nations) is strong evidence that Christ intended all true followers of Christ (not just the eleven remaining apostles) to be fully engaged in worldwide Great Commission work. If you are a Christian, how are you personally obeying Christ's command to make disciples of all nations?

_____

_____

_____

_____

7. The basic meaning of the word **disciple** (Gk. *mathetes*) is "a learner or follower of another." In the New Testament the word **disciple** is used to describe (1) unsaved Jews (John 9:28), (2) followers of John the Baptist (John 1:35; 3:25), and (3) followers of Jesus Christ. List four characteristics of a true or convicted disciple of Jesus Christ (John 8:31; Luke 14:26–27, 33).

_____

_____

_____

_____

It's time to order your next study. Allow enough time to get the books so you can distribute them at the Open House. Consider ordering 2-3 extra books for newcomers.

———————

ADDITIONAL
INSIGHTS

8. Jesus breathed on His disciples and said **Receive the Holy Spirit** (John 20:22). Many Bible scholars believe the coming of the Holy Spirit (His presence upon the church and His power) occurred on the Day of Pentecost (Acts 2:1–13) approximately fifty days later. If this is correct, what do you think Jesus meant when He said **Receive the Holy Spirit** in John 20:22?

_____

_____

_____

_____

9. Jesus' statement **If you forgive the sins of any, they are forgiven them; if you retain the sins of any, they are retained** (John 20:23) has led some to believe that God has granted certain individuals the privilege and power to forgive sins eternally. If this is the correct interpretation, however, it contradicts the clear teaching of Scripture that says God alone has the power to forgive sin (Mark 2:7; Luke 5:21). Since sinful man, however godly he may be, cannot forgive another man's sin, what do you think Jesus meant by this statement?

_____

_____

_____

_____

10. The apostle Thomas wasn't present the first time Jesus appeared to the disciples (John 20:19–24). When the rest of the disciples told Thomas they had seen the Lord, he said

he wouldn't believe unless he saw proof (John 20:25). Eight days later Jesus appeared to Thomas and the rest of the disciples (John 20:26–29).

a. How did Thomas respond to Jesus' exhortation (John 20:28)?

_____

_____

b. What encouraging words does Jesus offer all those who truly believe (including you, if you are a Christian) but have never seen the Lord Jesus in the flesh (John 20:29)?

_____

_____

11. Why was the gospel of Jesus Christ according to the apostle John written (John 20:31)?

_____

_____

_____

_____

TEN

DO YOU LOVE ME?

**Read John 21;
other references as given.**

At first glance John 20 could easily be the conclusion to the gospel according to John. Thomas, seeing the nail prints in Jesus' hands and the wound in His side, makes his epic declaration of faith **My Lord and my God!** (John 20:28). His declaration of faith could easily be considered the summary statement of John's gospel.

John 21 concludes this great book of the Bible, and it reads like a postscript to the rest of the book. It provides a compassionate interchange between the apostle Peter and Jesus and gives a glimpse of Christ's enduring love for those who have failed Him and His willingness to restore them to spiritual health and ministry.

Now, before you begin, please ask God to reveal Himself through His Word and to transform you into the image of His Son. May God bless your diligent study of God's Word.

Final Exam:

Are you meeting next week to study the Final Exam? To learn how to present it effectively, contact Lamplighters.

———

ADD GROUP
INSIGHTS BELOW

1. Jesus' trial and crucifixion and the initial post-resurrection appearances happened in Jerusalem. The words **After these things** (John 21:1) indicate an indefinite time had elapsed before Jesus appeared to seven of His disciples at the Sea of Tiberias (also known as the Sea of Galilee) (John 21:1). This third appearance by Jesus to the disciples (John 21:14) fulfilled His promise to meet them in Galilee (Matthew 28:10).

67

a. Peter, confused over the meaning of the Great Commission (John 20:21) and likely still disappointed over his own threefold denial of Jesus, decided to return to the fishing business. Six other disciples decided to follow him (John 21:3). What noteworthy event happened during their all-night fishing excursion (John 21:3)?

_____

_____

b. Peter, James, and John were professional fishermen (Matthew 4:18, 21). To them one side of the boat was the same as the other. Why did Jesus use this particular means (the catching of fish at His bidding) to reveal Himself at this time to Peter and the other disciples (John 21:4–6; Luke 5:1–11)?

_____

_____

_____

_____

_____

2. During Jesus' earthly ministry the disciples often misunderstood Him (Matthew 16:5–12; Mark 7:18). In the garden of Gethsemane they fled from Him (Matthew 26:55–56). During the trial Peter denied Him (Matthew 26:69–75). But when Jesus called out to the seven disciples in the fishing boat, he said **Children, do you have any food?** (John 21:5) Jesus used a Greek word (*paidia*) that means "little children" or "lads." It is a term of endearment and friendship. He also invited them to share a meal He had prepared (John 21:9–13).

a. What do you think Jesus' use of the Greek word *paidia* and His approach to Peter and the other wayward apostles teaches you about how to restore those who have failed in life?

_____

_____

_____

_____

Would you like to learn how to lead someone through this same study? It's not hard. Go to www.Lamplighters USA.org to register for *free* online leadership training.

b. Some Bible teachers use the story of Jesus' restoration of Peter and the other apostles as a biblical template for God's plan for reconciliation. However, they often fail to point out that reconciliation is not always possible. To what extent does God expect all believers to go to restore a broken relationship when the other person is unwilling to reconcile (Romans 12:18)?

ADDITIONAL
INSIGHTS

_____

_____

_____

3. The Bible records eight of Jesus' post-resurrection appearances. Religious liberals and other skeptics often refute the historicity of the resurrection, claiming many of Jesus' resurrection appearances were to His closest followers.

a. Who else saw Jesus after he was resurrected (1 Corinthians 15:1–8).

_____

_____

_____

b. The gospel writer Luke was a Gentile doctor who was not one of Jesus' closest followers during His earthly ministry. What did Luke say about Jesus' life and ministry after His resurrection (Acts 1:1–3)?

_____

_____

4. After Jesus and the disciples had eaten breakfast He asked Peter three times if he loved Him (John 21:15–17). Some Bible teachers believe Jesus' use of two different Greek words for love (*phileo, agape*) is important, but in the final analysis, Jesus' questions and Peter's replies are essentially the same.

a. Give at least two reasons why Jesus may have asked Peter the same question three times when Peter answered honestly the first time (Matthew 26:69–75; John 21:18)?

_____

_____

_____

_____

b. How was Peter to show Jesus that he truly loved Him (John 21:15–17)? Do you think this same principle applies to all believers, including you? Why?

_____

_____

_____

_____

5. Jesus began His public ministry by saying to His first disciples **Follow Me** (Matthew 4:19, Mark 1:17). He ended His earthly ministry by telling Peter the very same words (John 21:19). Today many Christians could be considered "cultural Christians." They claim to be Christians and go to church on Sundays, but they have no appetite for the Word, show only a slight concern for the lost, and manifest no observable evidence of the fruit of the Spirit. As one person said, "They (Christians) pray to God on Sundays, and prey on the rest of us the other six days."

a. If Jesus said to you, "Follow Me," what do you think He would expect you to do with the rest of your life?

_____

_____

_____

_____

b. What advice did Jesus give to Peter about following Him (21:20–23)?

_____

_____

_____

For more discipleship help, sign up to receive the Disciple-Maker Tips—a bi-monthly email that provides insights to help your small group function more effectively.

ADDITIONAL INSIGHTS

6. What affirmation did the apostle John make about the accuracy of the things he wrote in this gospel (John 21:24)?

_____

_____

7. The four gospels are God's divinely inspired record of the life and ministry of Jesus Christ. Together they comprise God's complete record of Jesus' earthly ministry. Nevertheless, John's gospel closes with these inspiring and thought-provoking words, **And there are also many other things that Jesus did, which if they were written one by one, I suppose that even the world itself could not contain the books that would be written. Amen** (John 21:25).

a. Which of the following individuals in John's gospel do you identify with most: (1) Nicodemus, the religious do-gooder who was lost but eventually came to faith; (2) the woman at the well, the sinner who tried everything, but was empty before Jesus saved her; (3) Peter, self-confident, but useless to God until he realized he couldn't do anything without Christ; (4) the Jewish leaders, religious but unbelieving, who said, **We have**

no king but Caesar; (5) Thomas, the religious doubter who needed more and more evidence but finally said, **My Lord and my God!**; (6) or someone else? Why?

_____

_____

_____

b. If Jesus asked you "Do you love me?" how would you answer His question?

_____

_____

_____

c. How has your understanding of Jesus Christ changed during this study of the gospel of John?

_____

_____

_____

What have you learned from this study of John's gospel that will likely affect the rest of your life?

_____

_____

_____

_____

LEADER'S GUIDE

Lesson 1: Behold, the King!

1. Mary took spikenard or nard, a very costly oil prepared from the roots and stems of an aromatic herb from northern India, and anointed Jesus' feet while He ate with the disciples. Since Jesus and the guests would normally be reclining at divans rather than being seated at a table, Mary's anointing of Jesus' feet would have been easily accomplished. She wiped Jesus' feet with her hair. Judas Iscariot criticized Mary's actions as wasteful.

2. Judas Iscariot was an apostle and also the treasurer for the apostolic group. He was also a thief. He carried the money box with him as they traveled, from which he regularly stole (the Greek imperfect verb tense signifies continuous action).

3. 1. She expressed her love for Jesus by offering a very costly gift to anoint Him.
    2. She expressed her love for Jesus by wiping His feet with her hair. Normally a Middle Eastern woman would not unloose her hair in public.
    3. She expressed her love for Jesus by touching His feet. Generally, an ordinary person would not touch a rabbi out of respect for him.
    4. She expressed her love by not allowing the social norms to limit her expression of worship.
    5. Other answers could apply.

4. a. David told Araunah he would not accept the piece of land as a gift. David said he would not offer the Lord anything as a burnt offering that didn't cost him anything.
    b. Answers will vary.

5. a. It was a great number of people who had come from the outlying towns and villages to celebrate the Passover Feast in Jerusalem. Although the Bible does not say, it is likely the people from Galilee that had seen the good things Jesus did in their midst.
    b. The disciples didn't understand Jesus was fulfilling a key Old Testament prophecy by entering into Jerusalem on a donkey.

6. Jesus said anyone who serves Him will be honored by the Father (John 12:26) and He (Jesus) would draw all people (all men) to Himself, including the Gentiles (John 12:32).

7. a. Jesus' humanity wanted to be saved from the crucifixion (Hebrews 12:2, the cross)—the time when He would be made sin for us (2 Corinthians 5:21). Jesus came to bear witness to the truth (John 18:37) and to seek and to save those who are lost (Luke 19:10).

   b. Rather than the Father granting Jesus' request to save Him from this hour (John 12:27), Jesus asked the Father to bring honor and attention (glorify Thy name) to His own name. To glorify God means to point others to God's person, power, and presence by all we think, do, and say.

8. 1. Satan's power has been broken forever (John 12:31).

   2. Christ's death on the cross (lifted up) is so effective that it includes all peoples, including the Gentiles. Perhaps Christ being lifted up has a "connection" with Moses who raised up an image of a serpent on a pole (Numbers 21:4–9). All those who looked at the serpent were healed.

9. a. To walk in the light means to follow Jesus' teaching as it is revealed in His Word the best you know how.

   b. Spiritual darkness (unbelief, confusion, etc.) will overtake you, and you will become unable to discern God's plan for your life.

10. a. God did not reveal additional truth (light) to them. This was in accordance with the prophecy God gave to Israel through the prophet Isaiah.

   b. God blinded the eyes of their understanding (he didn't allow them to understand anything else about Himself or His ways), and He hardened their minds (John 12:39). Hardening of their hearts means that God brought these people to the point that they were closed to God and His spiritual truths. In their own minds, they had closed their minds, but it was actually God who had refused to reveal any more truth to them.

11. The Word of God. In the immediate context it is the words Jesus spoke,

but, since Jesus is the Word, it includes all that God has revealed to man through the Holy Scriptures.

Lesson 2: The 11th Commandment

1. a. Answers will vary.
    b. Answers will vary.

2. a. Yes, Judas is a prime example.
    b. No, there is not biblical evidence of a believer being demon-possessed. However, believers can be oppressed or greatly influenced (taken captive, 2 Timothy 2:24–26) by demonic action when they allow habitual sin or spiritual strongholds to dominate their lives.

3. a. Peter was surprised and resistant to Jesus' attempt to wash his feet. Peter didn't understand the spiritual significance of what Jesus was doing.
    b. Jesus was saying that unless He cleansed Peter, he would have no true fellowship with Jesus.
    c. Everyone who is saved only needs to confess and repent of their present sin. They don't need to be saved again.

4. a. No. The cultural need for foot-washing at that time was clearly evident and not as applicable today. Moreover, there is no biblical evidence in the book of Acts or the epistles that foot-washing was practiced by the early church. Nevertheless, the act of washing another person's feet is a humbling experience for both people and strikes at one of the major sins in man—pride.
    b. Answers will vary.
    c. Believers will be blessed if they serve others. God always honors those who honor and obey Him. This blessing may be in the form of the immediate joy of serving or some future blessing from God.

5. a. Answers will vary.
    b. Answers will vary.

6. 1. Judas was careful to cover his real intentions (John 12:4-6).
    2. Jesus was careful to not disclose Judas' wicked plans (John 13:27).

3. Judas had a reason to be absent from the rest of the apostles, giving him an opportunity to work his wickedness (John 13:29).

4. Since Jesus chose the apostles, including Judas, it would have been logical for the rest of the apostles not to question Jesus' selection of him.

7. a. Jesus commanded the apostles to love one another to the extent that He had loved them.

b. All people, even the unsaved, will know who are the real followers of Jesus Christ. This is an amazing promise and a powerful evangelistic truth that the church needs to grasp. In a day when religious confusion and spiritual deception abound, the true church must learn to love others to such an extent that even the unsaved will say, "There is a true follower of Jesus."

c. Answers will vary.

8. Peter didn't understand that good intentions and human resolve weren't enough to be a faithful follower of Jesus Christ. He didn't understand a man may be willing to follow to do something noble, but the regenerate man still possesses a sinful nature that is contrary to the will of God (Matthew 26:41). Peter didn't understand that he must allow the Holy Spirit to control his life before anything good can be accomplished for God (John 6:63).

Lesson 3: Jesus Is the Way

1. 1. Jesus would go (leave them because of His impending death) and prepare a place for them (John 14:2).

2. Jesus would return and take them with Him to the place He had prepared (John 14:3).

2. a. Jesus said He is the exclusive way to God. Jesus said He is the way—not a way. Jesus said He is the truth—not another philosophical theory, an unproven thesis, or an unsubstantiated premise. Jesus said He is the life—not a philosophy for a better way of living. Jesus is the only way to God, the supreme truth within all creation, and the only One who can give eternal life. Jesus emphasizes this fact by saying no one can go to God the Father (in heaven) except through Him. Jesus could

not have answered Thomas's question more clearly and he could not have declared the exclusivity of getting to heaven more succinctly. There is no other way to God than through Jesus Christ.

    b.   Answers will vary.

3. a.   Answers may vary, but the biblical answer is *no*, based upon John 14:6 and many other passages.

    b.   Peter said there is salvation in no one else. He said there is no other name under heaven (other than the name of Jesus Christ) by which men must be saved (Acts 4:12). Man is either saved through trusting Jesus Christ completely, or he will be lost forever. There are no second chances after death, including reincarnations or suspended realities.

    c.   Paul understood that God wanted all men everywhere to repent (Acts 17:30). Notice there are no exceptions—**all men everywhere** (Acts 17:30). God had overlooked the spiritual ignorance or blindness of the men Paul was preaching to, but now that they heard the truth, they needed to repent. God had appointed a day—judgment day—in which He will righteously judge the entire world (Acts 17:31). This judgment will be done by Jesus Christ (v. 31, **the Man**).

    d.   Paul said they should be accursed (Galatians 1:8–9). The Greek word (*anathema*) is a very strong word that means damned forever. This is a solemn warning to everyone, clergy or otherwise, who tells others about how they can find acceptance before God.

4. 1.   Jesus told Thomas if he had known Him (Jesus) he would have been able to know the Father (John 14:7).

    2.   Jesus told Philip that the person who has seen (recognized the true identity of Jesus) has seen the Father (John 14:9). Jesus is the express image and representation of the Father (Hebrews 1:1–3).

    3.   Jesus said that He is in the Father and the Father is in Him (John 14:10–11).

    4.   Jesus said that the words He spoke were not His own words (words made up by Him as he lived and spoke), but the very words of the Father who did His works through Him (John 14:10).

    5.   Jesus said the works He did (sinless acts of righteousness) bore witness that the Father lived in Him (John 14:11).

5. What Jesus meant was that everyone who trusts in Him will do greater

works through the power of the Holy Spirit and prayer. Notice the reason that Jesus gives for being able to do greater works – He goes to the Father. This does not mean that believers will be able to miraculously feed 5,000 at one time, but it does mean that thousands may come to salvation through preaching and prayer. Not many days from this night, the Apostle Peter saw 3,000 come to faith at one time. This passage is a powerful reminder of the power of prayer and God's willingness to do more than they imagine.

6. 1. The first translation (KJV, NKJV) seems to imply human determination and devotion as an evidence of love for Christ. A believer will prove or demonstrate his love for Christ by his obedience to God's Word.
    2. The second translation (NASB, ESV) indicates a true or sincere love for Christ results in an obedient walk with God. If a believer focuses his attention on learning to love God, his life will naturally reflect God's love in a life of obedience.

7. a. The Holy Spirit.
    b. 1. The Holy Spirit's formal ministry began when Jesus Christ and the Father sent Him after Jesus' crucifixion (John 14:16, 26).
        2. The Holy Spirit abides with believers forever (John 14:16–17).
        3. The Holy Spirit is a Person (John 14:16; notice the word *He*).
        4. The Holy Spirit is called the Spirit of Truth. He always brings truth to light and exposes error (John 14:17).
        5. The unsaved (the world) cannot receive or understand the Holy Spirit (John 14:17). 6. The Holy Spirit is also called the Helper, and He teaches believers all things and reminds them of the spiritual truths they were taught previously (John 14:26).

8. 1. The Holy Spirit is referred to as He, which signifies personality (John 14:16–17). A force or attribute does not have personality.
    2. Peter said Ananias and his wife Sapphira lied to the Holy Spirit when they sold a piece of land and kept back part of the money (Acts 5:3). In the next verse Peter explains their sin and tells them that they did not (just) lie to man but to God (Acts 5:4). This is one of the strongest passages in the Bible to prove the deity of the Holy Spirit.
    3. The Holy Spirit is called the eternal Spirit (Hebrews 9:14). Eternality is an exclusive attribute of God, and the Holy Spirit partakes of that quality. This also is strong proof of His deity.

9. a. 1. If a believer loves Jesus, he will seek to know God's Word (has His commandments).
   2. If a believer loves Jesus, he will seek to obey God and His Word (and keeps them).
   3. If a believer seeks to know God's Word and seeks to be obedient to what God reveals to him, God will reveal or manifest more of Himself to the individual.
   b. The Jewish believers who were the recipients of the letter to the Hebrews had regressed spiritually. Rather than going on to spiritual maturity and learning the deep things of God (solid food), they had lost ground spiritually and were now dealing with simple spiritual concepts (milk).

10. God's peace transcends earthly circumstances because its confidence rests upon the character and promises of God. Since God is sovereign everything that happens to a believer has been sanctioned by God. Consequently, the believer can rest in this truth even though he may not like the difficulties that God allows to come into his life. The world's peace, on the other hand, is entirely circumstance-based. Since the unsaved cannot know God and His ways, they are not able to understand God's will.

11. a. Satan, indwelling in the hearts of wicked men (including Judas), was coming to accomplish his plan of killing Jesus.
    b. Even though Jesus was facing the darkest day of human history, unbearable suffering, and the temporary rejection of the Father, He was saying that he was prepared, and there were no strongholds of fear or unbelief that Satan could use to his advantage.
    c. Answers will vary.

Lesson 4: The True Vine

1. a. 1. God planted His vineyard on a fruitful hill (Isaiah 5:1). 2. He tilled the soil and cleared out the stones (Isaiah 5:2). 3. He planted the choicest vine (Isaiah 5:2). 4. He built a watchtower in the middle of the vineyard (Isaiah 5:2). He built a winepress in it (Isaiah 5:2). He planted the vineyard in hopes of reaping a good crop (Isaiah 5:2).
   b. 1. God lost hope that His vineyard would produce good fruit (Isaiah

5:3–4). 2. He took away the perimeter hedge that protected the vineyard (Isaiah 5:5). 3. He let the vineyard be burned (Isaiah 5:5). 4. He allowed the walls to be broken down and intruders to trample the vines (Isaiah 5:5). 5. He didn't do anything to repair the damage (Isaiah 5:5–6). 6. He allowed the vineyard to become overgrown with briers and thorns (Isaiah 5:6).

2. a. God chastens believers so their lives yield the peaceable fruits of righteousness (Hebrews 12:11).
   b. Answers will vary.

3. a. Love, joy, peace, longsuffering, kindness, goodness, faithfulness, gentleness, self-control.
   b. Answers will vary.

4. a. To abide in Christ means that the believer allows his mind and heart to be constantly controlled by God as revealed in His Word, and he is led by the abiding presence of the Holy Spirit.
   b. 1. The believer will bear much fruit (John 15:5).
      2. The believer will receive answers to his prayers (John 15:7).
      3. The believer will remain in the love of God (John 15:9–10). This means he will experience the abiding presence of God and the assurance of His love.
      4. The believer will experience God's joy during the normal trials and challenges of life (John 15:11).

5. a. 1. Believers are to love other Christians in the same way Christ loves them (John 15:12).
      2. Believers are to love other Christians to the point that they would lay down their lives for them (John 15:13).
      3. Believers are to love other Christians with a sincere love and fervently from the heart (1 Peter 1:22).
   b. The apostles could become Jesus' friends if they obeyed His commands (John 15:14). Jesus said they were called friends because He had disclosed all things that the Father had made known to Him.

6. a. In this context the world refers to those who are unregenerate and hostile to the ways and people of Christ. Those who are hostile to

Christ are guided by philosophies that are contrary to the teaching of Christ.

b. No, not in the same sense as the phrase *of the world* is used in this context. Believers live in or on the world (earth), but they are not part of the false system of beliefs that dominate the worldviews of the lost.

7. Answers will vary.

8. 1. Believers belong to a different family (God's family) that does not value the world's priorities (John 15:19).
   2. Christ prophesied that the world would hate His followers (John 15:19)
   3. The world hated Jesus and persecuted Him. It is natural that it will hate His followers (John 15:20).
   4. The world does not know God the Father, who sent Jesus Christ to this world (John 15:21).

9. Christians should not isolate themselves from the people that God has commanded them to reach for Christ. They should live godly lives in the midst of a sinful world so they can be a witness for Christ (Philippians 2:14–16).

Lesson 5: The Holy Spirit

1. a. They would be excommunicated from the synagogues and even martyred (John 16:1–2). Those who killed them would think they were serving God.
   b. The unsaved do not know God the Father or Jesus Christ (John 16:3), and the things of the Spirit of God are foolish to them (1 Corinthians 2:14).

2. a. 1. The Holy Spirit has personality (John 16:8).
      2. The unique ministry of the Holy Spirit during this present age began when Jesus left this earth (John 16:7).
      3. Jesus is the One who sent the Holy Spirit to His people (John 16:7).
      4. The Holy Spirit convicts of sin, righteousness, and judgment (John 16:8–11).

5. The Holy Spirit guides believers into all truth (John 16:13).

6. The Holy Spirit doesn't speak on His own authority but speaks only what He hears from the Father (John 16:13).

7. The Holy Spirit informed the apostles about the future (John 16:13).

8. The Holy Spirit points people to Jesus (John 16:14).

9. The Holy Spirit receives truth from Jesus and declares it to believers (John 16:14).

b. 1. The Holy Spirit convicts men of their sin, the righteousness of Jesus Christ, and His authority to judge all creation (John 16:8–11). Because Jesus' death on the cross brought judgment to Satan (the ruler of this world), He has the power or authority to judge everyone else.

2. The Holy Spirit is the One who applies the finished work of Christ on the cross to the account of those who trust Him completely for salvation. By one Spirit (the Holy Spirit) we are all (Christians) baptized or immersed into the saving work of Jesus Christ (Titus 3:5–6).

c. The unsaved, meaning all those who are unsaved.

3. 1. The Holy Spirit guides believers into God's truth (John 16:13).

2. The Holy Spirit does not speak from His own authority, but speaks whatever He hears from God the Father and Jesus Christ (John 16:13–15).

3. The Holy Spirit glorifies (seeks to reveal the person, presence, and power) of Jesus Christ (John 16:14).

4. a. 1. A Christian must not grieve the Holy Spirit (Ephesians 4:30).

2. A Christian must not quench the Holy Spirit (1 Thessalonians 5:19).

b. Grieving the Holy Spirit occurs when a believer resists the Holy Spirit's conviction about sinful thoughts and actions. Quenching the Holy Spirit occurs when a believer resists the Holy Spirit's prompting to do something that God wants the Christian to do.

5. a. To be baptized in the Spirit means to be immersed in the Spirit. This occurs for all believers at the time of their salvation. Notice the word we were all baptized … and have all been made to drink of one Spirit (the Holy Spirit).

b. Believers are commanded to be filled with the Spirit which means to allow themselves to be totally under the control and direction of the Holy Spirit.

6. It is likely # 3. Jesus was saying that the disciples would not see Him for a while (the time between His death and resurrection) and then they would see Him again during the forty-day period between the resurrection and His ascension.

7. a. 1. Answers to their prayers if they were prayed according to God's will (John 16:23).
    2. The fullness of joy that the believer can experience as a result of answered prayer (John 16:24).
   b. Answers will vary.

8. Praying in Jesus' Name means to pray according to God's will.

9. a. By faith in God which is manifested in the believer's life by obeying His Word.
   b. Answers will vary.

Lesson 6: What Would Jesus Pray?

1. a. Jesus immediately asked the Father for assistance so He could glorify the Father. Jesus' prayer is interesting because He immediately requested something for Himself, but His request was born in a desire to bring more glory to the Father. Believers would be wise to reevaluate their prayers and consider how many of their "personal prayer requests" are offered to God so that He might be glorified rather than presenting their prayers mainly for the fulfillment of their own desires.
   b. 1. It's not wrong to immediately request something from God. There are many examples of this in the Bible (David, Nehemiah).
      2. The things believers ask for themselves in prayer should bring glory to God. God knows what we need, and we can trust Him to provide that for us, but Christians should make sure their abiding desire in life is to bring glory to God in all they do and request (1 Corinthians 10:31).
   Other answers could apply.

2. a. Jesus' ultimate goal of dying on the cross was to give eternal life to as many as the Father had given Him.
   b. The definition of eternal life is that people would truly know the true identity of Jesus Christ and God the Father. This includes knowing all that God has done for them and receiving the gift of eternal life.

3. a. The goal of every believer's life should be to glorify God in all he does and says (Romans 16:27; 1 Corinthians 10:31).
   b. Answers will vary.

4. Jesus asked the Father to restore the glory that He possessed in eternity past (John 17:5, **before the world was**). When Jesus came to earth He humbled Himself (Philippians 2:8, yielded His active right to function as fully God even though He did not cease to be God) and took the form of a servant (Philippians 2:7). He was found in appearance as a man (Philippians 2:7), which means He took on humanity but not a fallen human nature. In doing this, Jesus voluntarily and temporarily laid aside the glory He originally had in eternity past so He could identify with mankind and accomplish the work of redemption. It is this glory that Jesus was asking the Father to restore to Him.

5. Jesus wanted His followers to know that everything He was and possessed (wisdom, grace, etc.) was from the Father (John 17:7). Jesus also wanted His followers to know that the Father and He were so intimately related that He makes no exclusive claim over creation or those whom the Father had given Him (John 17:2). Jesus' words reveal His claim to equality and unity with the Father (John 17:10). Moreover, Jesus and the Father (since they share completely) will be glorified through His followers.

6. a. 1. Jesus loved His followers and wanted the Father to preserve them (their salvation and sanctification) after His departure (crucifixion). Judas had been lost, and the Scriptures had been fulfilled (John 17:12), but Jesus did not want anyone else to be lost (Judas was a dead branch that was removed; John 15:2).
      2. Jesus wanted the Father to protect them from Satan's attack (John 17:15).
      3. Jesus wanted the Father to continue to set them apart from the world (sanctify them; John 17:17).

b. No. Jesus gives them eternal life at the time of salvation and He said they will never perish (John 10:28). Moreover, no one is great enough or strong enough to pluck them out of God's hand (John 10:29). Either the words *eternal life* mean what they say (eternal life), or Jesus gave a false promise.

7. a. 1. He prayed for them (John 17:15).
    2. He specifically asked the Father to keep His followers from Satan's attack (John 17:15).
    3. He asked the Father to sanctify them in the truth (John 17:17).
  b. Jesus sanctified Himself so His followers could have an example to follow.

8. a. Jesus commands His followers to make disciples of all nations (Matthew 28:18–20; Acts 1:8).
  b. God must preserve Christ's followers, and they must be sanctified in the truth.

9. Jesus prayed that all believers would be united in the same way that the Father and He are united (John 17:21). In John 13:34–35 Jesus stated this same desire at the beginning of the Last Supper with His disciples and here it is restated in a prayer to the Father. Both times Jesus gave the reason He wants believers to be united—that the (unsaved) world would know that the Father sent Him. Believers should strive for spiritual unity with other members of the body of Christ, but they must understand that God's desire is for unity, not unanimity. Jesus wants all believers to be unified in purpose and think and speak graciously about other believers, but he does not expect them to relinquish truth on the altar of ecumenical compromise.

10. a. Our union with God and the truth He has revealed in His Word.
  b. According to Webster's dictionary unanimity comes from Latin (*unus*—one, *animus*—mind) and means having the agreement and consent of all (such as "The decision was unanimous"). Unity means a condition of harmony or accord. It refers to continuity without deviation or change (as in purpose or action). Unanimity requires a group to come to a consensus opinion, and the group must speak as one unified voice. Unity, on the other hand, allows diversity of opinion while being united in purpose or cause.

11. Answers will vary but could include the following:
    1. A Christian should realize that Christ's command to be one with other believers is a command to be obeyed, not a suggestion to be considered.
    2. A Christian should realize Jesus' command is for him to love all other believers and be united with them and that can be done without forsaking the truth.
    3. A believer should love and respect other believers and churches without being critical of them.
    4. A believer should realize that God has not called him to be "God cop." Jesus said He would build His church and the gates of hell would not prevail against it.
    5. A believer should realize that no believer, including him, has all the truth of God.

Lesson 7: Betrayal in the Garden

1. a. Jesus approached Judas, the Jewish officers, and the Roman soldiers. This fact, often overlooked, proves Jesus was not hiding in the darkness and ultimately captured by the soldiers.
    b. The entire contingency of captors drew back and fell to the ground.
    c. Answers will vary. However, the Bible indicates the captors drew back and fell when Jesus said the words *I AM*. The very words (and perhaps the way He spoke them) are the reason they fell.
2. a. God said to say **I AM has sent me to you** (Exodus 3:14).
    b. **Before Abraham was, I AM.**
    c. The Jews took up stones to stone Him (John 8:59). They considered Jesus' use of the phrase I AM to be blasphemy (Leviticus 24:16) and worthy of death by stoning.

3. a. 1. I am the bread of life (John 6:35).
        2. I am the light of the world (John 8:12).
        3. I am the door for the sheep (John 10:7).
        4. I am the good shepherd (John 10:11).
        5. I am the resurrection and the life (John 11:25).
        6. I am the way, the truth, and the life (John 14:6).
        7. I am the true vine (John 15:1).

b. Jesus is saying unequivocally that He is God. Jesus is the true bread from heaven. God gave the Israelites quail (Numbers 11:31–33) and manna (Exodus 16:35) in the wilderness that gave them physical life, but Jesus is the true bread from heaven that gives eternal life. Jesus is the light of the world that dispels the spiritual darkness of sin. Jesus is both the door and the good shepherd (John 10:7, 11). He is the means by which His followers find safety and security, and He is the One who leads them to green pastures and doesn't leave them like a hireling. Jesus is the resurrection and the life. No one else is able to raise man from the grave. Jesus is the only way to God (John 14:6), and He is the true vine that gives life to every living branch that has been grafted in through salvation.

4. a. Peter, acting consistent with his impetuous nature, drew his sword and cut off the right ear of the High Priest's servant, a man named Malchus.

b. Jesus told Peter to put his sword away and said that he was able to bear the coming ordeal (crucifixion) that His Father had ordained for Him (John 18:11). Then Jesus asked permission to heal the man's ear and did so (Luke 22:50–51).

c. Answers will vary.

5. a. Peter denied knowing Jesus three separate times before the rooster crowed. This was a fulfillment of Jesus' earlier prophecy (John 13:38).

b. Peter went out and wept bitterly (Luke 22:62).

c. Answers will vary.

6. a. The Jews wanted the Romans to crucify Jesus by hanging Him on a cross (also referred to as a tree) rather than them stoning Him themselves. The Jews framed their case against Jesus by accusing Him of being an insurrectionist or traitor to Rome. Initially Pilate was not convinced that Jesus had done anything worthy of death and told the Jews to crucify Him themselves. Pilate knew the Jews would not crucify, Jesus so he was likely slightly mocking them by this statement.

b. Jesus became a curse (according to the Jews), but His sacrifice actually removed the curse of the Law (which is eternal death; Galatians 3:13).

7. Jesus was informing Pilate that He was a king, but said His kingdom was not of this world. Although all believers are citizens of heaven (Philippians

3:20), they, like the Jewish people for centuries, are citizens of a future nation. For the Jewish people, this happened in 1948 with the reformation of national Israel. For the believer, this happens when Jesus establishes His millennial kingdom at the end of the tribulation (Revelation 20:1–7).

8. Believers are (foreign) ambassadors for Christ (2 Corinthians 5:20). As ambassadors for Christ, believers are to be active in reconciling the world to Christ (2 Corinthians 5:21).

Lesson 8: It Is Finished

1. 1. They scourged Jesus (v. 1).
   2. They made a crown of thorns and placed it on His head (v. 2).
   3. They put a purple robe on Him (v. 2).
   4. They mocked Him by saying, "Hail, King of the Jews" (v. 3).
   5. They struck Him with their hands (v. 3).

2. a. The Jewish leaders thought Jesus was just a man.
   b. Pilate wasn't exactly sure who Jesus was, but he thought Jesus was only a man because he said, "Don't You know I have power to crucify You?" (John 19:10).
   c. Answers will vary. Answers will vary.

3. Pilate was afraid because his wife told him that she had suffered many things in a dream about Jesus. The dream revealed that Jesus was righteous (that just man). The dream had impacted her so much that she felt constrained to warn her husband not to have anything to do with Him (sentencing Him to death).

4. a. Pilate and the Jews possessed no power to harm or kill Jesus unless God sovereignly allowed it. God was not directing their actions, but He did allow sinful men to fulfill the desires of their hearts and accomplish His ultimate will—the salvation of man. The doctrine of God's sovereignty is one of the most profound doctrines in Scripture and provides immeasurable comfort to His people. God limits the expression of mankind's wickedness and allows them to express their wickedness only as far as His sovereign will permits.

b. God gives men the power to do evil in the sense that He sovereignly allows it, but this doesn't make Him the author of their sin. God has granted unregenerate mankind a limited expression of their will, including their desire to do evil, within the constraints of His sovereign will. God holds men accountable for their actions (eternal judgment) and uses their actions to work all things according to the counsel of His will.

5. a. You are "not Caesar's friend" (John 19:12). It is likely this singular statement, more than anything else the Jews said, is the one thing that made Pilate crucify Jesus. Pilate's career would not have weathered another Jewish delegation going to Rome and word getting to the suspicious Roman emperor.

b. We have no king but Caesar (John 19:15).

6. a. 1. The people ridiculed (sneered at) Him (Luke 23:35).
   2. The Roman soldiers mocked Him (Luke 23:36).
   3. One of the criminals who was crucified with Him blasphemed Him (Luke 23:39).
   4. Jesus suffered the shame of hanging naked before everyone who passed by (Hebrews 12:2).

   b. When Jesus died on the cross, He took away the believer's trespasses (sins) against God and made them spiritually alive (born again) in Him. He eliminated the list of past (and future) sins that had accrued against us (the handwriting of requirements against us) and eliminated them (having nailed them to the cross; Colossians 2:13–14).

   c. Answers will vary. Answers will vary.

7. The three words *It is finished* (John 19:30) are used to translate a single Greek word (*tetelestai*). Jesus said, *"It is finished,"* not "I am finished." Papyri receipts for the payment of taxes have been found with the words *tetelestai* written across them. The word is equivalent to "paid in full." Jesus was saying that the payment for man's sin—the act of redemption—was paid in full and complete.

8. 1. We receive the due reward for our deeds.
   2. This man has done nothing wrong.
   3. Lord, remember me when You come into Your kingdom.

9.

    a. Jesus was silent before   Isaiah 53:7
       Herod and Pilate

    b. None of Jesus' bones   Psalm 34:20
       were broken

    c. The Roman soldiers cast   Psalm 22:18
       lots for Jesus' clothes

    d. Jesus' side was pierced   Zechariah 12:10

    e. Jesus' hands and feet   Psalm 22:16
       were pierced

Lesson 9: He Is Risen!

1. a. Mary thought someone had stolen Jesus' dead body and taken it to an unknown location.

      b. Mary asked the gardener if he was the one who had removed Jesus' body. If he had, she would like to know where it was so she could take Jesus' body to another grave (John 20:15).

2. Believers must learn to take every thought captive to God's Word (2 Corinthians 10:4–5). This means the believer should intentionally challenge his own thinking and relinquish, by faith, any thoughts that are contrary to the Scriptures.

3. a. From a human perspective they didn't understand the biblical doctrine of the resurrection (John 20:9). From God's perspective, He had not revealed the doctrine of the resurrection to them (John 3:27). No one can receive spiritual truth unless God wills it (John 3:27).

      b. 1. A believer must have an understanding of God's Word (John 14:21, **has My commandments**).

          2. A believer must obey the spiritual truths God reveals to him (John 14:21, **and keeps them**).

          3. A believer must humble himself before God (James 4:6).

4. First, the linen cloths that Jesus' body was wrapped in were still lying there (John 20:5–6). It is extremely unlikely that someone or some people would

unwrap Jesus' body before they removed it from the grave. This would have (1) given the Roman soldiers more time to discover the thieves, (2) been unnecessary to transport the body, (3) made the body more difficult to transport, (4) exposed the bleeding wounds which would have left a trail of blood for others to follow and locate the body. Second, the small cloth that had been placed around Jesus' head was not lying with the linen cloths, but was folded and placed by itself (John 20:7). Thieves wouldn't have taken the time to fold the face cloth and lay it neatly away from the linen cloths.

5. Jesus wanted Mary and others to understand that there was now a change in His relationship with them. Since Jesus' resurrection, there was a new relationship and many of the old ways of relating had changed forever. No longer would Jesus walk among them as their teacher and friend. His presence with them was no longer His physical presence but through the abiding Holy Spirit. Jesus' disciples needed to understand this truth and make the transition in their thinking if they were going to experience continuing closeness to Christ

6. a. Mark 16:15 says believers are commanded to preach the gospel. Luke 24:47 says that repentance and remission of sins should be preached in His (Jesus') name. The gospel of Jesus Christ is the proclamation of man's need to repent and the promise of complete remission or forgiveness of sins. Repentance means a change of thinking about the consequences of sin and the true identity of Jesus Christ (God versus good teacher, etc.). The promise of God's complete forgiveness of sins is based upon Christ's death on the cross and gives those who repent the assurance of God's acceptance.
   b. Answers will vary.

7. 1. A true disciple abides in God's Word (John 8:31).
   2. A true disciple makes Christ the ultimate or supreme love of his life (Luke 14:26).
   3. A true disciple trusts Christ during life's most difficult challenges (Luke 14:27).
   4. A true disciple accepts his role as a steward or manager (rather than an owner) of the possessions God entrusts to his stewardship (Luke 14:33).

8. Jesus' giving of the Spirit was likely an initial bestowal of the Spirit's presence in the lives of the apostles in a limited sense to prepare them for the outpouring of the Spirit on the day of Pentecost a few weeks later (Acts 2). Perhaps Peter would have been bewildered during the day of Pentecost if this initial giving of the Spirit had not happened.

9. This difficult verse likely means that Jesus was bestowing the Holy Spirit on the apostles to enable them to discern those people who had truly repented and pronounce them saved. The apostles were likely given the Holy Spirit's presence to affirm decisions for Christ as genuine in a time of great confusion. Their position as apostles would have made them highly regarded and their words would have been taken with great weight.

10. a. Thomas said, "My Lord and my God!" Doubting Thomas, often the skeptic, was finally saved.
    b. Blessed are those who have not seen (Jesus in the flesh) and still believe.

11. The gospel according to John was written so that those who read it may believe that Jesus is the Christ, the Son of God, and that they will have eternal life.

Lesson 10: Do You Love Me?

1. a. Peter and the six other disciples fished all night, but they didn't catch any fish (John 21:3).
   b. Early in Jesus' ministry, He instructed Peter to move his boat to a different location on the same Sea of Galilee (also called the Lake of Gennesaret or the Sea of Tiberias), and this resulted in a boatful of fish (Luke 5:6). Peter, amazed by this sudden change of fortune, fell at Jesus' feet and said, "Depart from me, for I am a sinful man, O Lord!" Perhaps Peter immediately remembered the former event.
   Other answers could apply.

2. a. 1. Restoration of an erring believer or attempts to repair a broken relationship should always be done with gentleness and love.
      2. The person attempting to restore a relationship should offer

genuine gestures of friendliness that allay the other person of any fears of rejection, condemnation, or hostility.

3. Other answers could apply.

    b. God expects believers to do as much as possible to restore a broken relationship. The restorer should do everything he can to restore the relationship, but he must realize that it isn't always possible because the other person must be willing to restore the relationship as well.

3. a. Peter (Cephas), the apostles (the twelve), 500 believers at one time, James (the half-brother of Christ), and the apostle Paul (**me**, 1 Corinthians 15:8).

    b. Luke said Jesus appeared to the apostles and presented Himself alive by many infallible proofs over a period of forty days (Acts 1:2–3).

4. a. 1. Peter had denied Jesus three times so He gave Peter the opportunity to confess Him three times. Because God was going to use Peter mightily in the future, this would be important. Satan would have tempted Peter and reminded him of his threefold denial, and Peter would be encouraged to remember his threefold confession.

       2. Jesus prophesied that Peter would be martyred (John 21:18) and it would be important to Peter for him to remember that he made a bold confession of loyalty to Christ during his future trials.

    b. Peter was to feed Jesus' sheep and the lambs. This meant Peter was to care for Jesus' followers through the proclamation of the Word and shepherding them in their needs.

5. a. Christ expects all believers to relinquish their worldly goals and aspirations and wholeheartedly embrace His will for their lives as revealed in His Word.

    b. Jesus told Peter to keep His eyes off other people and God's plan for them.

6. John said he testifies that the things he wrote were true.

7. a. Answers will vary.

    b. Answers will vary.

    c. Answers will vary.

FINAL EXAM

Every person will eventually stand before God in judgment—the final exam. The Bible says, **And it is appointed for men to die once, but after this the judgment** (Hebrews 9:27).

May I ask you a question? *If you died today, do you know for certain you would go to heaven?* I did not ask if you're religious or a church member, nor did I ask if you've had some encounter with God—a meaningful spiritual experience. I didn't even ask if you believe in God or angels or if you're trying to live a good life. The question I *am* asking is this: *If you died today, do you know for certain you would go to heaven?*

When you die, you will stand alone before God in judgment. You'll either be saved for all eternity, or you will be separated from God for all eternity in what the Bible calls the lake of fire (Romans 14:12; Revelation 20:11–15). Tragically, many religious people who believe in God are not going to be accepted by Him when they die.

> **Many will say to Me in that day, "Lord, Lord, have we not prophesied in Your name, cast out demons in Your name, and done many wonders in Your name?" And then I will declare to them, "I never knew you; depart from Me, you who practice lawlessness!"** (Matthew 7:22–23)

God loves you and wants you to go to heaven (John 3:16; 2 Peter 3:9). If you are not sure where you'll spend eternity, you are not prepared to meet God. God wants you to know for certain that you will go to heaven.

> **Behold, now is the accepted time; behold, now is the day of salvation.** (2 Corinthians 6:2)

The words **behold** and **now** are repeated because God wants you to know that you can be saved today. You do not need to hear those terrible words, **Depart from Me ....** Isn't that great news?

Jesus himself said, **You must be born again** (John 3:7). These aren't the words of a pastor, a church, or a particular denomination. They're the words of Jesus Christ himself. You *must* be born again (saved from eternal damnation) before you die; otherwise, it will be too late when you die! You can know for certain today that God will accept you into heaven when you die.

These things I have written to you who believe in the name of the Son of God, that you may know *that you have eternal life.*

(1 John 5:13)

The phrase *you may know* means that you can know for certain before you die that you will go to heaven. To be born again, you must understand and accept four essential spiritual truths. These truths are right from the Bible, so you know you can trust them—they are not man-made religious traditions. Now, let's consider these four essential spiritual truths.

Essential Spiritual Truth

#1

The Bible teaches that you are a sinner and separated from God.

No one is righteous in God's eyes. To be righteous means to be totally without sin, not even a single act.

There is none righteous, no, not one;
There is none who understands;
There is none who seeks after God.
They have all turned aside;
They have together become unprofitable;
There is none who does good, no, not one.
(Romans 3:10–12)

...for all have sinned and fall short of the glory of God.
(Romans 3:23)

Look at the words God uses to show that all men are sinners—**none, not one**, **all turned aside**, **not one**. God is making a point: all of us are sinners. No one is good (perfectly without sin) in His sight. The reason is sin.

Have you ever lied, lusted, hated someone, stolen anything, or taken God's name in vain, even once? These are all sins.

Are you willing to admit to God that you are a sinner? If so, then tell Him right now you have sinned. You can say the words in your heart or aloud—it doesn't matter which—but be honest with God. Now check the box if you have just admitted you are a sinner.

◻ God, I admit I am a sinner in Your eyes.

Spiritual Death

Eternal Life

Now, let's look at the second essential spiritual truth.

Essential Spiritual Truth

#2

The Bible teaches that you cannot save yourself or earn your way to heaven.

Man's sin is a very serious problem in the eyes of God. Your sin separates you from God, both now and for all eternity—unless you are born again.

For the wages of sin is death.
(Romans 6:23)

And you He made alive, who were dead in trespasses and sins.
(Ephesians 2:1)

Wages are a payment a person earns by what he or she has done. Your sin has earned you the wages of death, which means separation from God. If you die never having been born again, you will be separated from God after death.

You cannot save yourself or purchase your entrance into heaven. The Bible says that man is **not redeemed with corruptible things, like silver or gold** (1 Peter 1:18). If you owned all the money in the world, you still could not buy your entrance into heaven. Neither can you buy your way into heaven with good works.

> *For by grace you have been saved through faith, and that not of yourselves; it is the gift of God, not of works, lest anyone should boast.* (Ephesians 2:8–9)

The Bible says salvation is **not of yourselves**. It is **not of works, lest anyone should boast**. Salvation from eternal judgment cannot be earned by doing good works; it is a gift of God. There is nothing you can do to purchase your way into heaven because you are already unrighteous in God's eyes.

If you understand you cannot save yourself, then tell God right now that you are a sinner, separated from Him, and you cannot save yourself. Check the box below if you have just done that.

☐ God, I admit that I am separated from You because of my sin. I realize that I cannot save myself.

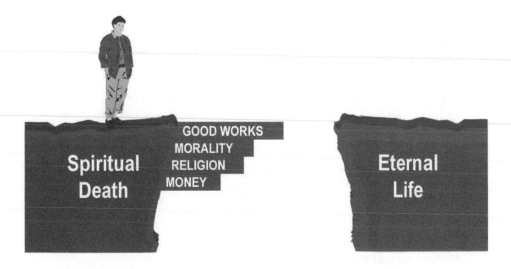

Now, let's look at the third essential spiritual truth.

Essential Spiritual Truth

#3

The Bible teaches that Jesus Christ died on the cross to pay the complete penalty for your sin and to purchase a place in heaven for you.

Jesus Christ, the sinless Son of God, lived a perfect life, died on the cross, and rose from the dead to pay the penalty for your sin and purchase a place in heaven for you. He died on the cross on your behalf, in your place, as your substitute, so you do not have to go to hell. Jesus Christ is the only acceptable substitute for your sin.

For He [God, the Father] made Him [Jesus] who knew [committed] no sin to be sin for us, that we might become the righteousness of God in Him.
(2 Corinthians 5:21)

I [Jesus] am the way, the truth, and the life. No one comes to the Father except through Me.
(John 14:6)

Nor is there salvation in any other, for there is no other name under heaven given among men by which we must be saved.
(Acts 4:12)

Jesus Christ is your only hope and means of salvation. Because you are a sinner, you cannot pay for your sins, but Jesus paid the penalty for your sins by dying on the cross in your place. Friend, there is salvation in no one else—not angels, not some religious leader, not even your religious good works. No religious act such as baptism, confirmation, or joining a church can save you. There is no other way, no other name that can save you. Only Jesus Christ can save you. You must be saved by accepting Jesus Christ's substitutionary sacrifice for your sins, or you will be lost forever.

Do you see clearly that Jesus Christ is the only way to God in heaven? If you understand this truth, tell God that you understand, and check the box below.

☐ God, I understand that Jesus Christ died to pay the penalty for my sin. I understand that His death on the cross was the only acceptable sacrifice for my sin.

Spiritual Death

Eternal Life

Essential Spiritual Truth

#4

By faith, you must trust in Jesus Christ alone for eternal life and call upon Him to be your Savior and Lord.

Many religious people admit they have sinned. They believe Jesus Christ died for the sins of the world, but they are not saved. Why? Thousands of moral, religious people have never completely placed their faith in Jesus Christ *alone* for eternal life. They think they must believe in Jesus Christ as a real person and do good works to earn their way to heaven. They are not trusting Jesus Christ alone. To be saved, you must trust in Jesus Christ *alone* for eternal life. Look what the Bible teaches about trusting Jesus Christ alone for salvation.

Believe on the Lord Jesus Christ, and you will be saved.
(Acts 16:31)

...that if you confess with your mouth the Lord Jesus and believe in your heart that God has raised Him from the dead, you will be saved. For with the heart one believes unto righteousness, and with the mouth confession is made unto salvation.... For there is no distinction between Jew and Greek, for the same Lord over all is rich to all who call upon Him. For "whoever calls on the name of the Lord shall be saved.
(Romans 10:9–10, 12–13)

Do you see what God is saying? To be saved or born again, you must trust Jesus Christ *alone* for eternal life. Jesus Christ paid for your complete salvation. Jesus said, **It is finished!** (John 19:30). Jesus paid for your salvation completely when He shed His blood on the cross for your sin.

If you believe that God resurrected Jesus Christ (proving God's acceptance of Jesus as a worthy sacrifice for man's sin) and you are willing to confess Jesus Christ as your Savior and Lord (master of your life), you will be saved.

Friend, right now God is offering you the greatest gift in the world. God wants to give you the *gift* of eternal life, the *gift* of His complete forgiveness for all your sins, and the *gift* of His unconditional acceptance into heaven when you die. Will you accept His free gift now, right where you are?

Are you unsure how to receive the gift of eternal life? Let me help you. Do you remember that I said you needed to understand and accept four essential spiritual truths? First, you admitted you are a sinner. Second, you admitted you were separated from God because of your sin and you could not save yourself. Third, you realized that Jesus Christ is the only way to heaven—no other name can save you.

Now, you must trust that Jesus Christ died once and for all to save your lost soul. Just take God at His word—He will not lie to you! This is the kind of simple faith you need to be saved. If you would like to be saved right now, right where you are, offer this prayer of simple faith to God. Remember, the words must come from your heart.

> **God, I am a sinner and deserve to go to hell. Thank You, Jesus, for dying on the cross for me and for purchasing a place in heaven for me. I believe You are the Son of God and You are able to save me right now. Please forgive me for my sin and take me to heaven when I die. I invite You into my life as Savior and Lord, and I trust You alone for eternal life. Thank You for giving me the gift of eternal life. Amen.**

If, in the best way you know how, you trusted Jesus Christ alone to save you, then God just saved you. He said in His Holy Word, **But as many as received Him, to them He gave the right to become the children of God** (John 1:12). It's that simple. God just gave you the gift of eternal life by faith. You have just been born again, according to the Bible.

You will not come into eternal judgment, and you will not perish in the lake of fire—you are saved forever! Read this verse carefully and let it sink into your heart.

> *Most assuredly, I say to you, he who hears My word and believes in Him who sent Me has everlasting life, and shall not come into judgment, but has passed from death into life.*
> (John 5:24)

Now, let me ask you a few more questions.

According to God's holy Word (John 5:24), not your feelings, what kind of life did God just give you? _____

What two words did God say at the beginning of the verse to assure you that He is not lying to you? _____   _____

Are you going to come into eternal judgment? ☐ YES   ☐ NO

Have you passed from spiritual death into life? ☐ YES   ☐ NO

Friend, you've just been born again. You just became a child of God.

To help you grow in your new Christian life, we would like to send you some Bible study materials. To receive these helpful materials free of charge, e-mail your request to **info@LamplightersUSA.org**.

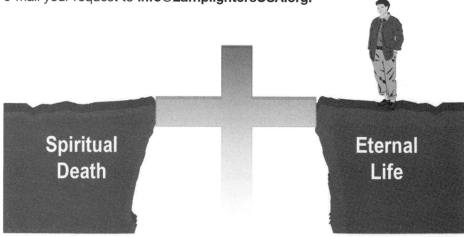

Spiritual Death

Eternal Life

APPENDIX

LEVEL 1 (BASIC TRAINING)
STUDENT WORKBOOK

To begin, familiarize yourself with the Lamplighters' *Leadership Training and Development Process* (see graphic on page 106). Notice there are two circles: a smaller, inner circle and a larger, outer circle. The inner circle shows the sequence of weekly meetings beginning with an Open House, followed by an 8–14 week study, and concluding with a clear presentation of the gospel (Final Exam). The outer circle shows the sequence of the Intentional Discipleship training process (Leading Studies, Training Leaders, Multiplying Groups). As participants are transformed by God's Word, they're invited into a discipleship training process that equips them in every aspect of the intentional disciple-making ministry.

The Level 1 training (Basic Training) is *free*, and the training focuses on two key aspects of the training: 1) how to prepare a life-changing Bible study (ST-A-R-T) and 2) how to lead a life-changing Bible study (10 commandments). The training takes approximately 60 minutes to complete, and you complete it as an individual or collectively as a small group (preferred method) by inserting an extra week between the Final Exam and the Open House.

To begin your training, go to www.LamplightersUSA.org to register yourself or your group. A Lamplighters' Certified Trainer will guide you through the entire Level 1 training process. After you have completed the training, you can review as many times as you like.

When you have completed the Level 1 training, please consider completing the Level 2 (Advanced) training. Level 2 training will equip you to reach more people for Christ by learning how to train new leaders and by showing you how to multiply groups. You can register for additional training at www. LamplightersUSA.org.

Intentional Discipleship
Training & Development Process

Multiplying Groups

The 5 Steps of Faith for Starting Studies

Training Library

Online Resources

Leading Studies

ST-A-R-T

10 Commandments

Solving All Group Problems

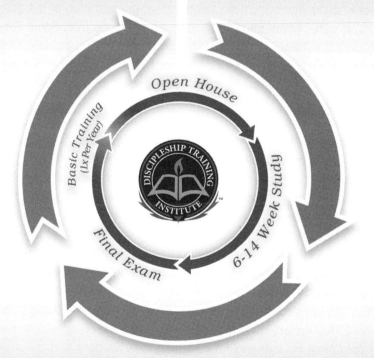

Open House

Basic Training (1x Per Year)

6-14 Week Study

Final Exam

Training Leaders

4 Responsibilities of a Trainer

Leadership Training

4 Levels of Student Development

3 Diagnostic Questions

John A. Stewart © 2017

How to Prepare a
Life-Changing Bible Study
ST-A-R-T

Step 1: _____ and _____.

Pray specifically for the group members and yourself as you study God's Word. Ask God (_____) to give each group member a rich time of personal Bible study, and thank (_____) God for giving you a desire to invest in the spiritual advancement of each other.

Step 2: _____ the _____.

Answer the questions in the weekly lessons without looking at the

_____ _____.

Step 3: _____and _____.

Review the Leader's Guide, and _____ every truth you missed when you originally did your lesson. Record the answers you missed with a _____ _____ so you'll know what you missed.

Step 4: _____ _____.

Calculate the specific amount of time _____ _____ to spend on each question and write the start time next to each one in the _____ using a _____.

How to Lead a Life-Changing Bible Study

10 COMMANDMENTS

1	2	3
4	5	6
7	8	9
	10	

Lamplighters' 10 Commandments are proven small group leadership principles that have been used successfully to train hundreds of believers to lead life-changing, intentional discipleship Bible studies.

Essential Principles for Leading Intentional Discipleship Bible Studies

1. The 1st Commandment: The _____ Rule.
   The Leader-Trainer should be in the room _____ minutes before the class begins.

2. The 2nd Commandment: The _____-_____ Rule.
   Train the group that it is okay to _____, but they should never be _____.

3. The 3rd Commandment: The _____ Rule.
   _____, _____, _____ ask for _____ to _____ the _____, _____, and _____ the questions. The Leader-Trainer, however, should always _____ the questions to control the _____ of the study.

4. The 4th Commandment: The ____:____ Rule.
   _____ the Bible study on time and _____ the study on time _____ _____. No exceptions!

5. The 5th Commandment: The _____ Rule.
   Train the group participants to _____ on God's Word for answers to life's questions.

1	2	3
4 **59:59**	5	6
7	8	9
	10	

6. The 6th Commandment: The _____ Rule.

    Deliberately and progressively _____ _____ participants into the group discussion over a period of time.

7. The 7th Commandment: The _____ _____ Rule.

    _____ the participants to get _____ the answers to the questions, not just _____ or _____ ones.

8. The 8th Commandment: The _____ Rule.

    _____ the group discussion so you _____ the lesson _____ _____ and give each question _____ _____.

9. The 9th Commandment: The _____-_____ Rule.

    Don't let the group members talk about _____ _____, _____ _____, or _____ _____.

10. The 10th Commandment: The _____ Rule.

    _____ God to change lives, including _____.

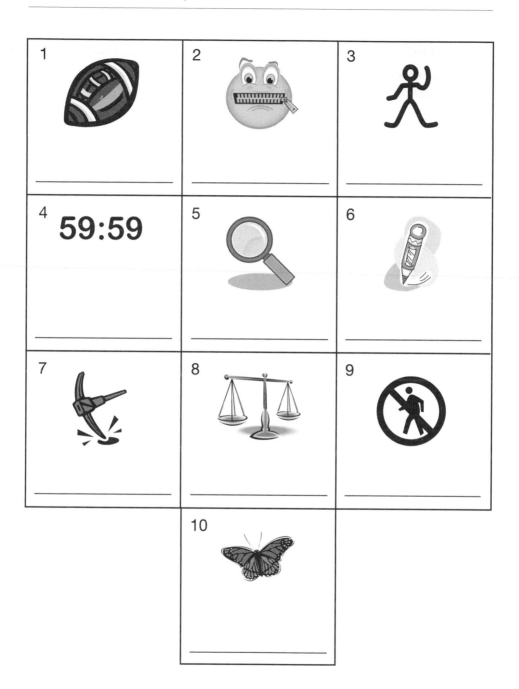

Choose your next study from any of the following titles

- John 1-11
- John 12-21
- Acts 1-12
- Acts 13-28
- Romans 1-8
- Romans 9-16
- Galatians
- Ephesians
- Philippians

- Colossians
- 1 & 2 Thessalonians
- 1 Timothy
- 2 Timothy
- Titus/Philemon
- Hebrews
- James
- 1 Peter
- 2 Peter/Jude

Additional Bible studies and sample lessons are available online.

For audio introductions on all Bible studies, visit us online at www.Lamplightersusa.org.

Looking to begin a new group?
The Lamplighters Starter Kit includes:

- 8 James Bible Study Guides
  (students purchase their own books)
- 25 Welcome Booklets
- 25 Table Tents
- 25 Bible Book Locator Bookmarks
- 50 Final Exam Tracts
- 50 Invitation Cards

For a current listing of live and online discipleship training
events, or to register for discipleship training, go to
www.LamplightersUSA.org/training.

Become a Certified
Disciple-Maker or Trainer

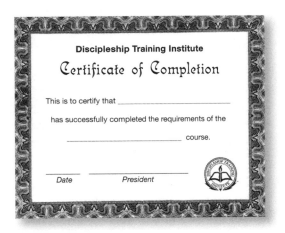

Discipleship Training Institute

Certificate of Completion

This is to certify that _____

has successfully completed the requirements of the

_____ course.

_____ _____
Date   President

Training Courses Available:

- Leader-Trainer
- Discipleship Coach
- Discipleship Director
- Certified Trainer (Level 1)

Contact the Discipleship Training Institute
for more information (800-507-9516).

The Discipleship Training Institute is a ministry of
Lamplighters International.